MEAN
MOMMY

MEAN
MOMMY

Tales of Motherhood Survival from the Comedy Trenches

Kerri Louise

Willow Street Press New York

For my mother : The loveliest, meanest mother of all.
Thank you for teaching me how to be a mean mother. I love you!

TABLE OF CONTENTS

ACKNOWLEDGEMENTS

First and foremost, the biggest thank you goes to my gorgeous and wicked funny, talented husband, Tom Cotter who made me the luckiest girl in the world when he said YES fourteen years ago and together we brought the three most amazing, awesome, and adorable boys into the world: Cameron, Harrison, and Tommy 2. This book would not exist without you and this wonderful journey we started together. Thank you for letting me tell our story and for supporting me every step of the way.

Thanks to my editors through the years of writing this book: Susan Konig, Denise Shillue, Kelly Haglund, Denise George, and Google.

Thanks so much to my wacky and longtime friend and very talented photographer Karl Baierlein. Thanks to Rik Sansone for the cover design.

Thanks to all my mommy friends who I annoyed by calling at odd hours to talk about my book.

Thanks for the support of my highly regarded comedian friends Susie Essman, Lisa Lampanelli, and Laurie Kilmartin.

A very special thanks to the woman who made it all possible, Susan Konig and Willow Street Press. It's because of you that I found my YES and that's all I needed!

Lastly, and most importantly thanks to my parents Elaine and George Mather, who taught me always to strive to be my very best and told me that I could be anything I wanted to be as long as I worked hard at it. And now, because of your loving dedication as the most wonderful parents ever, I'm an author.

WHO IS MEAN MOMMY?

Mean Mommy is a stand-up comic who got married and had three baby boys. Her husband is also a stand-up comic, so basically he's a kid himself, and that means there are four baby boys at home and they all want her breasts. *Mean Mommy* is tired. She's not even a real author. She just used writing this book as an excuse to get out of the house.

Welcome to *Mean Mommy* – she won't judge you. She'll just tell you you're doing it wrong, but in a funny, sweet, "you don't know it's coming" kind of way. *Mean Mommy*'s light-hearted, humorous stories about juggling a comedy career, a husband, and three boys will make you laugh so hard you'll pee your pants. Even though that's not saying much because most moms pee in their pants just by sneezing a little. Her attitude toward modern motherhood will entertain all mothers, including people who identify as being a mother. Her crass opinions are not for the easily appalled moms. Although it would do them some good if they read it. However, it's best that they don't because *Mean Mommy* is too busy with her own kids to be dealing with hate mail. This is an uncensored, totally honest blueprint on how to make your children sleep through the night, do unpleasant chores, and make them responsible for their own actions. *Mean Mommy's* tired of the "Everyone wins!" attitude. Let's all get back to the basics of parenting and cut the bullshit. With **Mean Mommy's** personal stories, her courageousness to think outside-the-box, and her straightforward advice, you'll be inspired, learn a few things, laugh and yes, possibly even cry, but not a bad cry – just an "Oh my God, I really needed to let that all out" kind of cry. If you're a mom who wants to have a positive experience without taking this whole motherhood thing too seriously, this book is for you. If you're a pregnant woman who wants to feel happy, excited, and confident for motherhood, don't read another chapter. But if you're a mom who wants to have well-behaved, well-adjusted, responsible children, all while looking fabulous on the soccer field, get a glass of wine and start reading.

You won't be able to put this book down. Okay let's be honest here, **Mean Mommy** has always been able to put a book down no matter how great it is. She's never, in her life, ever said, "I was up all night reading – I just couldn't put the book down!" So it's okay if you have to put this book down. She doesn't care. Her feelings won't be hurt. Just as long as you have a mommy brain fart and you forgot that you even bought the book in the first place and you buy it again. **Mean Mommy** suggests you keep the book on hand just in case, God forbid, you have to give your kids a good spank on the butt. Using the soft cover of course, not the hard cover. She's mean, but not that mean! Yes, she will even be so bold as to give you her opinion and talk about what everyone is too afraid to talk about, spankings. Along with other things like bed bugs, masturbation, hating your husband, and plastic surgery. *Mean Mommy* wants to be a great mom, but she doesn't want to lose who she is in the meantime.

Mean Mommy is your best friend. She'll tell you like it is – in terms you can understand. Like she will tell you exactly how old her children are. Not this, "Oh my baby is 79 weeks old" kinda shit! What is that? "Okay, 4 weeks goes into one month, so one month divided by 12! What?! Don't make me do Math! I don't even care how old your baby is – I was just making conversation. So put down that gluten-free, homemade baby food for a second and talk to me like a real Mom!"

God knows *Mean Mommy*'s no doctor, and she doesn't even come close to one of your really smart friends, but she'll be the one you turn to when you've come close to alcoholism, drug addiction, and basically just going insane because you know she's been there, too. *Mean Mommy* will comfort you by saying, "Yes, it's okay to let your child watch TV so you can finally take a second to catch your breath, do the laundry, and empty the dishwasher."

You will be the hero if you suggest this book for the next read in your book club. They'll actually read it and not just show up for the free wine. It's like your therapy session only cheaper. Why do you think *Mean Mommy* wrote this book? She needed a good, long, free psychotherapy session. So *Mean Mommy* hopes that after reading this you feel so good about yourself that you'll cancel your Tuesday afternoons with Dr. Therapist Face.

Mean Mommy is not like these other moms, "Oh it's so rewarding having children." Who are these mothers anyway? *Mean Mommy* hasn't received a reward yet! Her kids are a little older now and she's still waiting for her rewards. *Mean*

Mommy's kids have rewards and trophies for shit they just participated in – they didn't even win! *Mean Mommy* drove them there! Where's her reward? You know when she'll get her rewards? When her kids are changing her diapers.

Mean Mommy's kids are in bed on time. Not because it's best for her children to have a good night sleep, or that she's this perfect mom, but because her favorite sitcom is starting and she doesn't want to be interrupted.

Mean Mommy gets back to the fundamentals of parenting. Basically, she cuts through all the bullshit and gets down to just plain common sense to parenting. Screw all this politically-correct parenting crap. She will remind you that you're a mother for a reason and that instinctually you already have what it takes to be the best mother you can be. She is your voice of reason. *Mean Mommy* is a real mom with real problems who is not afraid to admit what they are. You'll learn with her, you'll laugh with her and most of all she will be your new BFF. One you don't ever have to call, send a card, or invite over for a play date. Which is a relief. Right? 'Cause you couldn't handle another play date where you have to pretend to like your friend's kids. All you have to do is follow her on Twitter, like her on her Facebook page, or whatever the social media that's popular by the time this book is published.

Basically this book is a bitch session of *Mean Mommy's* inner thoughts, and she hopes you're able to go along for this wild ride. So buckle up and hold on tight, but don't feel guilty if you decide that this ride's not for you. You can always use this book as coaster for your Pinot while you binge watch *Orange is the New Black*.

Or to help start a small campfire. #bringmarshmallows

WE PLAN, AND GOD LAUGHS

I wanted all my ducks in a row before I had kids. Like every little girl, I dreamed that my husband and I would have the perfect house with the beautiful baby room all ready and waiting for the new arrival. It would be painted pink with the big letters of her name over the crib with matching baby quilt and crib bumpers (before they were outlawed). There would be a rocking horse made of responsibly farmed, sustainable wood in the corner next to the window seat where I would read to her. The nursing glider would be right next to the window, too, so I could look out and see the beautiful landscaping of my back yard while I'm doing what is referred to as "the most natural thing in the world." You get the picture...the room looks like page 32 in last month's Pottery Barn catalog.

So here was my plan... I'd be a stand-up comedian for a while and live it up in New York City. I'd soon get discovered, be cast on a successful sitcom and become famous. I'd get married to a successful, handsome, famous someone. We'd have an awesome home with a huge playground in the back for my four beautiful kids. Two boys, two girls, alternating the sex with exactly two years between them starting with the boy first named after his father of course. All before my thirtieth birthday.

Here's what really happened... I'd been a struggling comic for about 12 years until I finally got married to another struggling, handsome comic in my thirties. Six months later I thought my eggs were going to dry up, so I panicked and we got pregnant.

It all started soon after we got married. I had my husband Tom move in with me because I was living in a rent controlled building. It was a one bedroom, six floor walk-up apartment in New York City. Yes, six floors. I moved there because it was cheap and I was young. I loved living there because I felt safe. Who was going to rape me after climbing up six flights? Can you picture the rapist getting to the top? Pointing the gun to my face and saying, "Ok you do it, I'll watch."

Besides, I was going to be rich and famous SOON, so the six flight walk-up would be a great story to tell on "panel" – that's industry talk for when I would be a guest on Jay Leno.

After a month of living as newlyweds in the six-floor walk-up, we decided to go to Hollywood to get famous. We had each other now! We were funny! And we were going to give it that old college try. We rented a one bedroom in Santa Monica for three months. We both had great representation at the time and we thought this would be a good investment and lots of fun. #workinghoneymoon.

We thought that this would be our time to finally get discovered after all these years. Tom's manager was the same person who managed Ray Romano from *Everybody Loves Raymond*. His agent was The William Morris Agency, which is arguably the best agency in the world. My manager handled some of the best comics like Tim Allen and Drew Carey. So it was a no-brainer. We were in the best hands and this would be our moment! We'd get jobs on sitcoms and we'd have health insurance and we could finally start to build our family. Right? NO!

My husband and I didn't have any auditions. We thought our phone was going to ring off the hook, but we got nothing. I mean NOTHING. No calls.

Looking back now, those three months in Hollywood were some of the best times of our lives. Don't you wish an angel would come down and tell you to drink in this moment because these are going to be some of the best years of your lives? No one ever tells you those things! You have to wait for years and then when you look back, you say to yourself, "Wow I should have paid attention, I should have relished in those moments. I should have eaten more ice cream." We were young, and in love and in Los Angeles where the sun always shines and it was beautiful. Yet we still complained about what we didn't have, but looking back now we had a lot. First of all we had each other, and that's really all that matters. (Aw, did that make you wanna throw up a little?)

We complained about our agents and we complained about the lack of auditions, all while living the life. Yoga in the middle of the afternoon! By the way, yoga is a law in LA. You can't stay in L.A. for more than three days without doing a yoga class or they'll kick you out. I'm not kidding they will literally buy you a plane ticket home. Tom and I would go to the Santa Monica Pier almost every day. We would walk, run, or rollerblade. We rented bikes. We would go to the movies at the Third Street Promenade with all our comedy friends.

We would love to take these long lunches at the Thai place around the corner. Now, I can't remember the last time I took a long lunch or even sat down to eat my lunch. Eating with two hands – another thing no one tells you that you'll miss. My favorite place to go after yoga class was The Coffee Bean & Tea Leaf. (Think Starbucks but with the possibility of someone famous walking in with big sunglasses on.) I never minded the time it took to stand in that line and order a large, steamed something that I couldn't afford, but I did it anyway. God, what I would give to have the time to wait in that long line again. Then at night, we would get to make people laugh in some of the most prestigious comedy clubs in Hollywood. Every now and again we would get invited to our managers' lavish parties and we would run into some famous people. This was the life! It felt like our honeymoon never ended, but I didn't know that then. We still thought we were struggling and trying to make ends meet. I didn't know that this moment in time was really something extraordinary and it would never be the same again. In the midst of the lazy days in L.A., we got a little bored. We got tired of waiting for fame to find us – so we decided to try to make a baby. We wanted to wait just a few more months before we started to try, but we thought, well, no one ever gets pregnant right away so let's just do it. #sticktotheplan

Right out of the gate, first time ever not using any kind of birth control. Not only did I get pregnant, but I got pregnant with...wait for it...twins. We just didn't know it yet. #firsttimesthecharm

How does that saying go? We plan, and God laughs! It's true you're never ever going to be ready for kids. Nothing's going to be perfect, so stop trying to get it that way. Having the perfect baby room doesn't guarantee you'll even have a baby! Nothing will ever prepare you for what you are about to undertake – you just have to do it and you will get by, you will make it happen and it will be beautiful, just the way you didn't plan it.

Here's how fast this happened. We have sex, I mean we made sweet, romantic love like we've never made before in our whole lives. At least that's how I'm going to remember it. We conceived for God's sake, I have to remember it that way.

After a week or so, Tom had to leave L.A. to do a few road gigs and we planned to meet each other back home in New York. I actually had to extend my stay for the three days so I could do the one and only audition I got the whole three months I was out there. No, the audition couldn't have come earlier when I was doing nothing but the downward dog position. We both went out there to get famous and all we got was pregnant. #ThanksLA

So Tom goes to his gigs on the road and I go to my audition. The next few days I get pregnancy boobs! I swear I grew two sizes. At least I think they're pregnancy boobs, I don't know... I've never been pregnant before! Plus I was late. Not to my audition, but I was late for my period. I was probably a little late to my audition, too because L.A. traffic sucks. So now, I really think I'm pregnant. Instinctually, I know I'm pregnant, but I wanted to find out with my husband, and he's on the road.

Next day, the phone rings and it's a callback to that audition. They want to see me again. Now whenever I get callbacks to any audition, I get so nervous that I usually screw it up for myself. Not this time! I was so concerned that I may be pregnant that getting this job was the least of my concerns. I was not worried about what the producers of the show thought of me, or how important this role was, or that I had to be better than that pretty be-atch in the waiting room. I was focused on leaving L.A. and finally meeting up with Tom so we could find out together if we were pregnant. Bottom line – I killed it at the audition. Okay, the pregnancy boobs may have helped a little. #boobsrule

I promised Tom that I would not take a pregnancy test and I would wait for him so we could take it together. I waited two days for him to come home. That's like 16 days in "Holy shit, I might be pregnant" time. I wanted it to be romantic and I wanted to find out together. Finally, he comes home and that night we're reading the directions to the pregnancy test. The test that had been on my desk staring me in the face for two whole days. So the directions say if you see a blue line you're pregnant and if you see a white line you're not pregnant. It turned BLUE! *Then Tom ran and got the white out.* We were thrilled! We were excited! We were scared!

I made an appointment with my doctor the very next day.

My husband had an unexpected audition, so he couldn't go with me to my doctor's appointment. Yeah, I know...where was this audition when we were sitting around doing nothing but downward dog and having sex in L.A.? And don't performers ever skip an audition? Um, no.

The doctor did a sonogram and I saw on the monitor something that looked like a little diamond ring and he said, "See that diamond ring type thing? That's it!"

Then he moved the sonogram and I saw another diamond ring and I said, "That looks like another diamond ring."

And he said, "Hmm, that's interesting."

As soon as he said that I knew I was having twins. I was laughing, crying, and feeling very awkward with my legs spread wide open and a penis shaped camera with a condom on it was inside me. *Where was that condom when I needed it?*

We wanted this to happen. We just didn't think it was going to happen on the first try and we never even dreamed of having two. My husband will tell you that he has always dreamed of having twins, *but they were the Olsen twins and that's a different story all together.*

I was "diagnosed" with twins when we were living in a one-bedroom, six floor walk-up apartment in New York City with no health insurance, and we were still paying for our so called "business trip" to Hollywood. Again, NOT the way I planned it.

I left the doctor's office literally shaking. It felt like I had butterflies in my stomach and I kinda did – two of them! I was thinking about how I was going to tell my husband that we're having not one baby, but two, as I walked by a store with balloons filling the windows. One, in this big bunch of Mylar balloons, said "Twins!" and I thought, that's perfect.

Then my big cell phone with an antenna rang (before smart phones). It was my manager telling me I got the part from the audition I did in L.A. with my pregnancy boobs!

Note to self: if you want to nail an audition, get pregnant.

For years I'd been waiting for this opportunity. For years I'd been dreaming of having kids, but wanted to get my career off the ground and now the same day I find out my life will never be the same, I finally get the news I've been waiting for my whole career.

Then I threw up under a tree, on a city sidewalk, right on a sign that said, "Curb your dog."

I ran back to my one bedroom, six floor walk-up apartment to tell my husband the happy news, and *the other* happy news, AND THE OTHER happy news.

"It's true we're pregnant!"

Then I gave him the balloon. "With twins??!!" he said.

Oh and another little thing... "I got my first TV show and they want me back in L.A. this weekend for filming." The next thing he said was, "Does this job come with health insurance?"

We just held each other in disbelief and cried a little and then laughed a little, then cried again. Then laughed a lot saying, "This can't be happening!"

That night when all was still, I could hear God laughing so hard he was crying, too.

MY AMNIO SACKS ARE JOINED AT THE HIP

I had to keep my pregnancy a secret at least until I finished filming this TV show. So after a weekend filled with me hobnobbing and trying to fake drink with all the produces and VIP executives from the network, the show never saw the light of day. Like every actor before me, it was the big break that wasn't. Yes, another disappointment in a long line of many too boring to go through but this time the sting wasn't that hard even though it was my biggest break. If I didn't have two little things growing inside of me, I probably wouldn't have gotten out of bed for about two weeks after that devastation. I had quickly forgotten all about that "Big Break" that I'd been wishing for my whole career. All because I had a more important role. I was about to be cast in the role of my life or as I would like to call it the "Mother of all Roles." I was going to be a mother of not one, but two and I had to be prepared. I had to know what my motivation was for my new character. I had more important things to do. So, I immediately went out and picked up the script. You guessed it – *What to Expect When You're Expecting.* #What?MyCharacterCan'tDrink!?

The very second you make that big announcement that you're having a baby, you're getting judged as a mom. Yes they're saying they're happy for you, but deep down inside you know they're judging you...

"Oh my God, do you think they actually planned this?"

"They live in a one bedroom apartment."

"Is she going to quit her job?"

"I thought she looked a little FAT!"

When I told people I was pregnant the first thing that most of them said was NOT, "Oh I'm so excited for you!" or "Congratulations!" No, the first thing they said was, "Wow, what are you going to do?" As if I just got a life threatening disease.

Well, come to think of it, there are times that you could look at motherhood like that, but still. Why can't I be a mom and still be a comic? What do they mean, "What am I going to do?" I'm going to be an awesome mom who's going to follow her dreams. My dreams are not going to get a death sentence because I'm pregnant. What were they expecting me to say? "Well, I'm going to quit being a comic, stop dreaming, and get a real job, because people are hiring newly pregnant woman, nowadays."

But I didn't say any of that! I wanted to, I just panicked and smiled and said, "I don't know." Don't you hate it when someone pisses you off and, when you finally think of that clever come back, they're gone! That's what Twitter is for #yousuck! Or you can always write a book like me.

So, getting back to all this negativity I felt among my family, friends, and colleagues. I should be happy, but why do I notice a dark cloud hovering over me, as little disapproval raindrops start beating me on the head. I shook it off because I was going to prove them all wrong. I was going to be *SuperMom*! We're all like that in the beginning, right? You get every book on "What to expect," "What's your embryo doing now", and all the "how to" parenting books, too. You download every app that had the word baby in it! Yes, throughout your pregnancy you're going to read every single one of those informative books, websites, and blogs. They will tell you all the things you need to do to be prepared. But in the end you find yourself asking the question, "Why do I feel clueless after reading these? Why do I feel like I've failed as a mom already and my fetus hasn't even grown fingernails yet? Oh my God, will I be able to stop drinking coffee? It's going to be hard to kick my happy Cosmo friend out of the house. What's this prenatal vitamin I gotta take every day?" You start hallucinating that the light coming from the computer screen is really the Wizard of Oz in 3D and it's yelling at you to, "STAND BACK, STAND BACK and get off this computer, the light waves are giving your unborn child an extra set of eyeballs."

Then you start thinking of all the things your mother's been telling you and that she may be right:

You should really have a career before you get pregnant.

You're not ready to have kids yet; you don't even have a savings account.

You know your life will never be the same, NEVER.

Stop snoring!!

Okay, my mother didn't say the last one. My husband did.

I had so much information in front of me on how to be the greatest mother in the world. And even if you're not looking for information. these companies track you down. I got flyers and pamphlets through the mail. How did these people know I was even pregnant?

I got one flyer about stem cell banking. They take your child's umbilical cord and freeze it so if anything should happen later in life and you need it, you'll have your child's stem cells. It's expensive and you have to pay for it every year.

This was yet another thing to scare my already emotional, weary pregnant mind. My husband said, "We don't need that. We got the child we've always wanted and one for parts." So I said, "We'll just do it ourselves. When you cut the twins' umbilical cords just take two little zip lock baggies with you. We'll freeze them ourselves. You just gotta take the good zip lock bags, not the ones from the dollar store. The ones where you can write what it is and the date. Because I don't want you ten years later saying, What? I thought they were fish sticks!"

I downloaded a daily calendar according to my due date and every day I would read it and it would tell me exactly what was going on in my body. One day it read, your fetus is six inches from head to rump. Now I have to double it. I yelled to my husband, "Honey, I have two six inches inside of me right now, isn't that exciting?"

He said, "You know what's even more exciting? You're getting a third one tonight!" So if you're newly pregnant don't go insane with all that information out there. Take it easy save your energy for when the kid finally comes out of you, you're gonna need it.

While I was pregnant with the twins people would always ask us, "Did you get pregnant with twins, by using fertility drugs?"

Not unless you count Prozac and tequila as fertility drugs.

Due to my high risk pregnancy I had to take an amniocentesis test. They take a huge needle, stick it in your belly and suck the amniotic fluid from your child's amnio sack. Then they test it to see if your baby has Down syndrome. So that's two huge needles in the belly for me. TWO! I don't know why but I took the test – in hindsight I shouldn't have taken it!! I mean I'm 6 months pregnant for God's sake at this point I just couldn't bear to hear that the twins were joined at the hip or even worse, that one of the twins has a tiny, foot growing out of his head. It caused so much anxiety and stress and isn't that bad for the baby? What would I do with that information?

Then I think to myself, I want to know. I have to know. I want to know because then I can be prepared and together my husband and I will have a choice. What choice would we make? The bottom line is that, I DON'T KNOW. Sometimes I think we know too much and we have too much technology and it's a bad thing. God doesn't give you anything you can't handle. Then I think well, God made the smart people who came up with this technology so you can "handle" the information, so why not take it and do the right thing. What's the right thing? I don't know and I'm so glad I never had to find out. So in hind-sight would I take this amnio test again? I DON'T KNOW! I didn't get one for my next pregnancy and I was five years older.

It was seven days after my amniocentesis test and I was six months pregnant, but looking more like eight, I had to fly to Texas to work a comedy club with my husband, Tom. I was nervous because I was not sure it was safe for me to fly five days after taking two huge needles into my amnio sac. The doctors assured me it was fine, but being a new nervous mom I was, well, nervous.

Suddenly Tom came down with gout in his foot and couldn't walk. We didn't know it was gout at the time we just knew he was in a lot of pain and couldn't walk. By the time we landed in Dallas, Tom was incapacitated. So picture a very pregnant woman, carrying two bags on her back, pushing her husband in a wheelchair and pulling a suitcase behind her. All the while keeping that cell phone in her hand so the doctors could call with the results of the amniocentesis test. I starting praying, "Please, God let the phone ring with good news because at this point I just can't even fathom the idea that my twins could be in a wheelchair for the rest of their lives – I can't even bear pushing my husband along in one right now!"

We finally got into the rental car and I started driving because Tom's foot had to be elevated. We were hoping that his foot would stop hurting soon and that it probably had something to do with the flight. I turned to back out of the rent-a-car parking lot and I twisted my belly and I felt a sharp pain. Normally that would be fine, but since I just had the amnio, plus I'm all freaked out about the flight, and my husband is now in a wheelchair, I had a panic attack. I thought I had ripped the amnio sack or something like that. I stopped the car at some dreadful rest area and I ran into the bathroom and cried. It wasn't a cry that you do at sad movies or a sad commercial when you're getting your period (I hate when that happens by the way) – it was a cry like none I've ever experienced before. I was crying while breathing and heaving while trying to catch my breath. I couldn't control myself. Hyperventilating, crying and sobbing like a mental patient. I kept telling myself to get it together, and the more I tried to pull it together the harder it was to breathe. That 15 minutes in the bathroom took everything out of me. I scared myself and the poor woman who came in just to wash her hands. She probably wanted to go the bathroom, too, but she just freaked and left.

I got back to the car and tried to tell Tom about my little incident. He couldn't believe this was happening to me because up until now I'd been so calm throughout my pregnancy. I said, "We have to stay here. I can't drive I need to just sleep." I crawled into the back seat of our Kia rental car barely fitting myself and my babies. I managed to get comfortable and just crashed. I slept like a baby with potential genetic abnormality. Two hours passed and I was still sleeping. Tom managed somehow to get behind the wheel and, with his bad foot, started driving us to the gig – at rush hour.

We managed to do the show despite the excruciating pain my husband was in and the emotional pregnant state I was in. We made the nice folks in Texas laugh and the next day, we finally got the news that the twins were fine. What a relief and before you know it the tears staring rolling down my face again. We also found out that Tom didn't have to amputate his foot. He just had gout and there's a pill for that.

Unfortunately there are no pills for emotional pregnant ladies.

MEAN MOMMY ON TIME OUTS

That's right mommy needs a "time out" with her sippy cup filled with vodka. I'll just sit in the corner and be quiet for five minutes with my "Mommy Juice." Wouldn't it be nice if mommies could get "time outs"? No, we never get time outs and we're the ones who need them most. They say that time outs should last as long as your child's age in minutes. So if you have a five-year-old, the time out should last five minutes. Wouldn't it be nice to sit for 35 minutes with absolute quiet? Okay I'm older than that, but if I told you my real age you would be like, "Oh my, that's too long for mommy to sit in the corner!" So, I'll just leave it at that.

THE SHOW MUST GO ON

You might not understand the mind of a performer and you may never understand and I don't blame you. We're deranged, psychopathic, and just plan cuckoo. After two decades, my mother still thinks this is a hobby of mine and she's still waiting for me to get a "real job." So I will explain it to you the best I can – Tom and I have never called in sick to a gig. Don't get me wrong we've been sick as dogs, but as performers, we know that as soon as they announce your name nothing else matters. Your adrenaline takes over and no matter how sick you are for that 35 minutes or however long you have to tell your jokes, something takes over and you get it done. You're a performer and "The show must go on!" So even if you're tired, sad, cranky or sick, you somehow get the job done, and as soon as you get off that stage you go right back to being tired, sad, cranky or sick again.

I've driven for five hours in a snowstorm when it should have taken me only two. I was risking my life because I was afraid to say no to a gig. I never wanted a booker to ever think I couldn't do it. I never wanted a booker to ever think that

I'm not easy to work with, that I was not reliable, or that I was too chicken to drive in a snowstorm. Besides I'm a New Englander – I can drive in the snow with my eyes closed, but that's not the point. The point is we stop at nothing to get to a show on time.

One time, driving to a gig in New Jersey, I was stuck in traffic so I called the club to tell them I would be a little late and the booker just yelled at me saying, "Get here as fast as you can!" I was so afraid I would never work that club again, that as soon as I got out of traffic I gunned it. I was driving so fast I got pulled over got a $200.00 ticket. That was way more than I was even making for that night. Anyone in their right mind would have turned around and gone home after that. Not me, I still drove like a madwoman risking another ticket and again my life just to try to get to the gig on time. In my mind there are so many comics just waiting for the opportunity to step in at any given moment and I couldn't let that happen – ever. You can't always control the audience laughing at your jokes, but you can control being reliable, easy to work with and competent. No matter how big or small a show was. No matter how little they were paying me or even if it was one of those free audition shows I always seem to end up doing, I never called in sick.

I'll never forget working a gig in Portland, Maine with my husband, Tom, who was my boyfriend at the time. Tom drove up from New York on Thursday to do a show and radio the next morning. I had a gig in the city that night so I was going to take the bus and meet him the next day. I had to teach aerobics that morning (how else am I going to pay for my comedy career?) so I took the earliest bus I could get after teaching that class. It was a tight connection, but all sweaty, I made it just in time to argue with the guy who wanted to put my bag under the bus. I said, "No, I'm going to bring it with me." He said I couldn't because it was too big.

Reluctant to give him my bag, I finally said okay and got on the bus. Later I kept thinking that was really weird that he wouldn't let me take my bag on the bus and I actually never saw him put my bag under the bus. I looked around and there were bags bigger than mine on the bus. I had a bad feeling about this and I suspected he might have stolen it. Sure enough when the bus pulled into the rest area, I checked and my bag was gone. Holy crap, all my performing clothes were in there, I have nothing to wear to my shows all weekend. I couldn't perform in what I had on. I was in a sports bra, t-shirt and leggings soaking in my sweat. My really expensive curling iron was in there, too. My hair was going to look like shit all weekend.

I called Tom right away to tell him the news. I told him that he had to go shopping for me to get me something to wear for the show tonight and that he had to get me a bra. "A what?" he says. "You got to be kidding me. You want me to get a bra for you?"

"You have to!" I said. "There's no time for me to do it when I get off the bus I only have time to shower, change and go to the show!" So for the next half hour I was trying to explain to him what the letters and the numbers mean on a bra and what an underwire looks like. Whatever you do, don't get those lift me up, extra padded bras. My boobs are big enough I don't need a floatation device around my neck. Then for the next two hours I was thinking about how stupid I was to give that ugly guy my bag. I was yelling at myself really loud (in my inner voice) to always trust my instincts. Making a note to myself to always watch the guy actually put your bag under the bus! You idiot! Every ten minutes or so I would think of what got stolen and I would get even more mad at myself. My favorite perfume. My grandmother's necklace. I can't replace that!

The bus comes to a stop and the bus driver says, "Portsmouth." I'm so excited that we're here and hour early, that I'm not paying attention to where we are. All I keep thinking was, now I have time to go shopping and get a fairly decent bra because I don't trust Tom to get me the underwire I so desperately need. You can't be funny with your boobies hanging down by your knees. I run off the bus and into the nearest clothing store I see. I call Tom as I walk in there telling him I'm an hour early and to come pick me up. I'm getting clothes and I will meet him in front of the store. I'm so busy trying on pants that I don't even realize that I got off at the wrong bus stop, nor did I realize that I was in the wrong state! I was in Portsmouth, New Hampshire and I had to be in Portland, Maine for a show that started in an hour. The phone rings and I'm in the changing room. It's Tom: "I can't find you or the store. There are no clothing stores here! Kerri, are you sure you got off on the right stop?"

And then it hit me, "I'm in the wrong place."

"Kerri, the show starts in an hour and you're in another STATE!!"

"I know!" I said, "Oh My God! I know!"

"Get in a cab now!" he says "I'll hold the show up as long as I can, just get here." I ran out of the changing room, paid for the clothes, hopped the nearest cab and told him to drive as fast as humanly possible. In the meantime I clean my sweat with the wipes I made with tissues and sanitizer. I manage to peel my sports bra off, put on the new bra, without the cab driver seeing anything. (Thanks, *Flashdance!*) I had my makeup in my pocketbook – thank God that didn't get stolen. That's worth more than ten curling irons. I put my make up on, finished getting dressed, and called Tom to tell him I'm two minutes away. He said he will take his time introducing me and that I should just run out of the cab and onto the stage and that's exactly what I did. To this day my husband still makes fun of me for that brainless move. Every time I do something stupid he says well at least you didn't get off a bus in A DIFFERENT STATE!

And I would have had to do at least four weekends at that club to break even to what that cab ride cost me.

So you get the picture – we will stop at nothing to get to a gig. Having kids is no different. When the babysitter calls in sick I gather my kids in their PJ's and take them to my show, trusting that the comics I'm working with are not drug addicted assholes and will watch my kids while I'm on stage. Then I fire the sitter the very next day. She obviously doesn't have the passion for babysitting, like I have for my career! #You'reFired (Is that still even funny?)

MEAN MOMMY ON SPANKINGS

I've spanked my kids. There I said it. Not only did I say it, I just wrote it. There's no denying it. I can hear the knock on the door now, "Hello, it's the department of social services. We just want to come in and take a look around." Why is this a taboo subject? I could count how many times I've spanked my kids on one hand, *if I was holding a calculator,* but still. (I'm kidding, that's my husband joke, anyway) My husband is in favor of spankings. *Not for the children, but he likes to spice up our love life.* I'm not a supporter of spankings nor do I condone them as a regular form of punishment. But what I'm saying is, if you find yourself in a situation and you give your child a little swat on the hiney, please don't kill yourself over the fact. That's not teaching him to be aggressive. Some of the most aggressive kids I have ever seen are from homes that don't use any discipline at all. Maybe, and all I'm saying is just maybe, that little brat needs is a smack on the butt every once in a while. This politically correct crap has gone way too far to put fear in parent's heads that spankings are the most terrible thing you can do to a child. Most of our parents did it and we're fine. I think we should all get back to the basics. Don't ask your child, tell your child. Don't reason with your child, bribe your child, or let them rule your life. You are the parent – you need to lead your child. You're not your child's friend. It's your responsibility to set boundaries, tell them right from wrong, and make sure they take responsibility of their own actions. Your children will hate you for it now, but they will thank you for it later. If your child doesn't scream, "I hate you!" at least once in their lifetime then you haven't done your job. At the same time, you have to make sure your child knows he's loved unconditionally. You have to make sure they know they are wanted, valued and respected. That's a hard thing to do and it's hard to find that balance, so good luck with that. You've got to let your children know they're loved unconditionally while you're grounding them. #NoHateMailPlease

DON'T LET THE BEDBUGS BITE

I moved eight months pregnant with twins from a six floor walk-up on the Upper East Side of Manhattan to Harlem. Yes, that right – Harlem. That's what white people do when they're planning a family – they move to Harlem. (Think the opposite of *The Jeffersons.*)

It was the closest place to the city that we could afford with an elevator. When I say I moved us. I mean, I moved us. I did all the packing and everything while my husband was working on a cruise for nine days. It sounds bad because it was bad. I will never do that again. I will never move eight months pregnant again! EVER! #ManwithaVan

The Upper East Side was nice but very snobby; a lot of really rich people that wouldn't even give you the time of day. Even the homeless guys wouldn't talk to you. Harlem was nice – everyone was helpful. I remember being a new lonely mom, down and out, so sleep deprived, looking like crap, smelling like spit up, and all I wanted to do was just get the twins out of the house. I would walk the boys down the street and everyone would talk to me. "Look at you, SEXY MOMMA! I'll babysit for you anytime." People wanted to help me in Harlem. Even the homeless guys talked to me, "Are those twins? God bless you and the twins!" I mean they were spitting all over my boys, but at least they were blessing them. It got so bad I had to put the rain guard over the stroller even though it wasn't raining. *Then all the homeless guys wanted to squeegee it.* We loved our little place in Harlem.

And it was anything but! It was huge to us. Coming from a one bedroom, six floor walk-up apartment to a three bedroom, elevator, brand spanking new building! It was awesome. We had a doorman! My address was Madison Avenue NYC. I know, right!? I felt like I was someone special until I walked out of my building and realized I was living in one of the most crime-ridden areas in New York. At one time, this was basically one of the worst neighborhoods in Manhattan, a place to avoid at all costs and here I am standing in the middle of it with my two children. I kept telling myself that this was an investment and a good move and that we were part of gentrifying Harlem. We were right. We never would have been able to afford our home in the suburbs if it weren't for us moving to Harlem. In fact, we can't even afford to buy our old place now and the new building across the street is asking for millions for a studio apartment. We loved every bit of our experience in Harlem except this one time...

You know that little saying: "Good night don't let the bedbugs bite!" I used to think that was a cute expression that you would say to your kids before they went to bed, until those little eensy-weensy, teeny-tiny bed bugs were sucking the life blood out of me. These minuscule blood suckers aren't stupid. They knew who to suck the life out of and they did for nearly five months. They would crawl over my cold blooded husband to get to me, the hot blooded pregnant woman with twins. During the whole third trimester of my pregnancy and beyond, I kept on getting this rash and I looked like a pregnant woman with the chicken pox.

Every gynecologist, dermatologist, and doctor I saw said, "Oh, it must be some kind of a pregnancy rash. The good news is that it will go away as soon as you give birth!" So I would scratch all day and night and wait in agony until the birth of my children. One dermatologist said I had dry skin and that I had to take long baths and lubricate. Then he gave me a hand out on how to hydrate your skin. I said, "Are you sure? It looks like these raised little bumps are all in a row as if they were bug bites?" He looked at my big fat pregnant belly and wanted nothing to do with me, and he said, "I'm positive." This all happened way before bed bugs were even a thing, before anyone knew that they actually exist. Before they were even popular! We all thought they were fake little things that people made up for the poem we tell the children. That's why we never thought it was, in fact, bed bugs. Especially when my husband didn't have any bites on him.

After I gave birth my rash didn't go away. I was afraid to pick up my little baby twins and hug them because I thought my oozing rash might be contagious to them or hurt them in some way. I had the baby blues in ways you could never imagine. All the pictures of me holding my babies for the first time are all pictures of me with this awful, disgusting red rash all over my face and body. Granted women never look good hours after giving birth, but my pictures took it to a whole new level. I looked like a sumac victim with leprosy holding two little babies. One of the reasons why I stopped breast feeding was because I thought that the hormones were still running through my body and it was still causing this rash.

There was this one special night that I was really looking forward to going to. My husband got booked to open for Olivia Newton John and I couldn't wait to go see her sing live! For those young millennials reading this, Olivia Newton John was every little girl's idol in the movie *Grease*. Think Miley Cyrus! The Miley before she went crazy and started twerking.

My mother-in-law came to babysit so I could go to the show with Tom and everything would have been perfect if I hadn't been scratching my whole body all day. I scratched so much I put scars on my body and I had this one particular bite right on my nose. It took me so long to try to cover it with makeup and then I would scratch it, then it would bleed and then I would have to try to cover it up again. It was just awful. I got all dressed up for this black tie affair and I tried my best to be in a good mood. I really wanted to have fun and I was so looking forward to this event and I was so proud of my husband. This was an important gig for him and I didn't want to screw it up by being late or whining about my rash. The sad thing is that I don't really remember her singing. All I remember was how ugly I felt. I wasn't feeling good either so I left the party early. I went back home put cream all over my face, and cried my eyes out while I was sitting in the very bed the bed bugs were biting me.

Finally my mother-in-law, who is a nurse, told me to see a dermatologist and demand an autopsy. While waiting three days for the autopsy results, Tom came home very late from one of his gigs, put the light on in the bedroom and actually saw a little bug on our bed. He woke me up, we took one look and that was the moment where it all came together for us. It was bed bugs that have been destroying our lives for five months. It was bed bugs that have been snacking on me on a nightly basis. It was bed bugs that stole the joyful moments of the first few weeks of my twins' birth. These weren't just any bed bugs, they were Harlem bed bugs. Which means there were gangs of them and they all had guns, box cutters and knives. They smoked cigarettes. The very next day I researched bed bugs and got all my answers.

These little critters took us for thousands of dollars. We had three different kinds of exterminators, threw out luggage, got rid of furniture, got a new mattress, slept on the worst pull-out couch for two weeks and we did loads and loads of laundry in very hot water. It was soon after this episode that there was this bed bug epidemic in New York City. Now every exterminator specializes in bed bugs. Everyone knows about them now and everyone knows that they really, truly exist. In fact, I think we were the ones who started the whole bed bug craze in New York. So, you're welcome! By the way, why would you say, "Good night, don't let the bed bugs bite!" to your child right before they go to bed? Sleep tight, but don't let creepy, crawly things suck your blood and leave you for dead like they tried to do to Mommy before you were born. #Wehadbedbugs1st

MEAN MOMMY ON SLEEPING THROUGH THE NIGHT

I s the baby sleeping through the night? I don't know if he's sleeping though the night, but I am. That's the important thing. Mommy needs her beauty sleep.

As soon as the doctor says you can get rid of that middle of the night feeding – DO IT. Here is where you need to become the *Mean Mommy.* Let your baby cry it out! The crying will get to you, but if you can survive it for at least three nights of hell, your child will be sleeping through the night and you will, too. Have lots of binkies for him to suck on, don't break down and feed him. Trust the doctor who says babies have plenty of reserve to sleep through the night. The more they sleep, the better you look. The more they sleep, the more they sleep. So never wake a sleeping baby!

Make sure you put them in their crib right before they fall asleep so they know that's their place to sleep. If you transfer them after they sleep they will not know how they got there and what the bed is for. That little mobile above the crib is there for a reason. That will remind them it's sleepy time.

HE'S GETTING EVICTED THROUGH
THE SUN-ROOF

I loved performing pregnant and soon it was going to end. In the early stages of pregnancy, performing when no one knew you were pregnant was weird. I was at that tired, slap happy, silly stage of pregnancy, which if you had a real job they would fire you or ask you to go home, but in my job it only got funnier and better. Then when I had the big belly I loved performing even more. Before I even open my mouth I could feel the audience loving me and they couldn't wait to hear what I had to say. I've never felt that feeling before. I would always have to spend the first five minutes of my act proving myself to the audience. Trying to get them to like me. It happens as I'm getting introduced, I would walk up on that stage and I could just feel the audience hating me before I even said my first joke. I could sense them judging me and thinking women aren't funny, she doesn't look funny, what's she doing up there? But being pregnant I felt like they were already on board, like I could say anything and they would laugh. It was an awesome feeling. I would wobble up there with my big, fat, funny looking belly... look around and say, "So, I was fucking this guy right?"

Something about a pregnant, foulmouthed woman is so funny and I had so much fun with it, and now it's gone and I miss it. #GetAPropBelly

It was getting close to the due date and we didn't have our baby names. Well, we had three picked out if they were both girls or boy and a girl. But if they were both boys we were at a loss for the second boy name. My husband said what about Zachary for a name and I screamed, "'ZACHARYYYYYY ZACH! Get in the house Zack.' Yeah that name works, I like that name." Tom said, "That's how you test out a name - by yelling at our unborn child?"

I did that joke on stage so much when I was pregnant I got sick of that name so that was crossed off the list. My twins were conceived on Easter Sunday back in L.A. I know, don't tell my mom, we should have been at church, but we were on our knees some of the time and I think at least one of us said, "Oh My God!" So what's the difference? My due date was Christmas Day. I'm not making this up. So basically I'm looking at this like I'm the Virgin Mary! Anyway, I'm figuring if the twins are born on Christmas Day and I give birth to a boy and a girl I can name them Mary and Joseph. "JESUS, MARY AND JOSEPH GET IN THIS HOUSE NOW!" See, those names work! We went back and forth so many times on these names.

It was hard enough to pick one name for one baby and we had to pick six combinations of names. Finally we decided on our way to the hospital in the gypsy cab we got from Harlem at 5 in the morning after my water broke. "What if it's two boys – what do you want the second boy name to be? I like Harry. What do you think?"

Tom said, "Well, do you think he will get made fun of in school because our last name is Cotter. Harry Potter rhymes with Harry Cotter?"

"No way!" I said, "By the time he's in school that won't even be popular." Fast forward to years later and Universal Studios has dedicated a whole amusement park to Harry Potter. Our family actually paid thousands of dollars for my son Harry Cotter to ride Harry Potter and the Forbidden Journey five times in a row while my little one cried on my lap the whole time because he wasn't tall enough. Thanks Universal! #funtimes #not

Oh and by the way my twins did not make it to their due date. They came early, *just like their father.*

V-back, C-sections, Baby A and Baby B – are we learning the alphabet or are we in the delivery room? I had my twins via C-section. That's not how I had it planned out, but baby B wouldn't turn around and was breached. If we waited any longer for something to happen my doctor was leaving for the day. Yes, the doctor that I saw every two weeks for nine months. The doctor that I fell in love with because he was going to deliver my two babies safely. The doctor that I had trusted to put gadgets up my mommy parts and look around was going to just leave me, just like that. After all that time we had together, he was just going to leave because his shift was over and some unknown who has never seen my vagina before was going to take over. I don't think so! So he said we can have the babies out in 45 minutes or you can wait all day in labor and maybe the baby B will turn once baby A is out or some unknown doctor can go up there and try to turn your baby around which may end up in an emergency C-section anyway, your choice? Needless to say, I chose the C-section in 45 minutes.

The operation went fine and the babies were healthy and beautiful. It was after that where there were some complications. I've heard of preeclampsia during pregnancy which is basically getting high blood pressure and is common in a woman's first pregnancy and if she is carrying twins. If left untreated it could result in a poor outcome for mother and or baby. Luckily I didn't get that, but for some reason I got it right after I delivered the twins. I thought I was fine, but then I never left the recovery room and then when I saw the nurse put a third bag of some kind of liquid going through my IV up on one of those metal stick holder thingies with the wheels on the bottom. (I don't know what they call that thing. I never got into any of these medical drama shows like *Grey's Anatomy* or *ER*.) But you know what I mean. When that happened I thought, hmm maybe I'm not all right. Three bags on that metal thing had to mean something bad. Later my husband told me I was in the recovery room for 11 hours. I was all drugged up it felt like two minutes. I had no idea I was that bad. All I remember was the doctor telling the nurse that I had to take some kind of medicine and that she could give it to me under my tongue or up the butt and then I kindly, but firmly interrupted them and said, "Um, Mrs. Nurse, I can take it under my tongue. Yeah, I'm sure I can do that just fine – my tongue is fine – I'm able to do that." After that I was begging for water and the nurse said she could only give me ice chips. I promised and begged her like a drug addict that I would drink the water really slow. I think I even said to her Girl Scout honor and held up my two fingers. I really was going to do that. I wanted to keep my promise. The poor nurse could have lost her job for giving me that water, but I don't know what came over me. I got that water and I chugged it so fast you would have thought David Copperfield was in the delivery room with me making it disappear. No sooner than that I threw it all up. I immediately raised my hand and yelled to all that could hear me, "That was my fault! No worries I'll clean it up. My fault! I drank the water! I'm sorry! She told me not to and I didn't listen, I'm so sorry. I'll take the ice chips now. You were right."

MEAN MOMMY ON THE THREE DAY RULE

Remember three days because it's going to come up in this book a lot. Why? Because I believe it takes about three days for most anything. It's my THREE DAY rule. It should only take three days to change a kid's bad habit. Of course it will be three days of living hell, but a lifetime of happiness will follow. However, your husband's bad habits could take up to a year, and most likely they'll never get fixed. As long as you stick to your guns and stick to the plan at hand, use the proper tools and reinforcements and you should be able to get rid of the habit. Obviously every habit and every kid is different so it may take more than three days. It may take three hours, three months or three years. Either way my point is this – if you can last at least three days then don't stop, you're well on your way to success! It takes about three days for any boo-boo or bruise to heal. I always say to my kids, "Wait three days it will get better." Before I bring my kids to any emergency room I wait three days. That's if they don't have a bone sticking out of their body and they're not bleeding profusely or cracking their skulls while running around naked.

AND ON THE THIRD DAY HE ROSE AGAIN!! #justsaying

WHY CAN'T YOU BE MORE LIKE YOUR BROTHER!

When people find out that both my husband and I are comedians, they say, "So your twins must be really funny?" Yeah, in the delivery room I could have sworn I heard one twin said to the other, "Hey, two guys walked into a womb..." My twins are not identical, thank God, because then we would have had to tattoo one of them. It was still hard to keep track of them. Especially in the beginning with the feedings. I had to remember who ate first, which one pooped, and did I just give the same baby a bath twice? People thought I was crazy. I had daily charts and graphs recording what everyone was doing or I would have forgotten to feed one of them. My husband hated filling out those charts, "I have to write down how his poop looked? Really?" "Yes," I'd say, "I need to know how it looks to make sure he's not sick and if he is getting enough food." I even had a chart for me. Did I take my medicine; was I sleeping when the twins were sleeping? Was I eating and pooping enough? Mommy had to be healthy, too. "Honey, do I really have to write down what your poop looks like, too?"

"No, honey, you can leave that blank just check it off that it was done!" We should have had a chart like that for my grandmother when I was younger. I remember my mother would ask her at least 10 times a day, "Did you move your bowels today?" Then she had to repeat it louder because my grandmother was hard of hearing. A chart could have come in handy during that awkward moment at the Italian restaurant. They probably have an app for that, now. If they don't, I should come up with one and go on *Shark Tank*. #DidYouPoopTodayApp

Having twins has made me lose my mind as you can see from reading this book so far. It was a life changer and a challenge like no other. People would always ask me how I do it and I never really had an answer for them. Someone said to me, "God doesn't give you anything you can't handle!" So I guess I was able to handle it. Your motherly instincts just take over. You don't have time to think about how hard it is or how much work it is. You don't think about how you're doing or if you're doing it right, you just try to keep these two little precious things alive the best way you can, all while trying to survive yourself. You just do it. It helps that they're so damn cute and, when they smile, it's a feeling like no other. That's what carries you through.

The little itsy, bitsy smile or laugh that gets you through your whole day. And I get two of those!! I think it also helped that I didn't have one baby first, then the twins. I had two right off the bat so I didn't know any better. I just thought this is how it goes.

I guess the real answer to "how do you do it" is: Be Organized. It's not like I'm this organized person. It just happened because if I didn't get them on the same sleep routine, I would never sleep. So I don't think it was because I'm just the perfect organized mommy, I just needed and wanted my beauty sleep! I'm selfish. So I worked hard at making sure they were on the same schedule and on a really good routine, which coincidentally is the best thing for the baby anyway. "Everyone eats, sleeps and poops together, or else!"

It wasn't always easy. One day I decided to try to breast feed my twins at the same time. I was sleep deprived. I didn't have the common sense to know that if I was having a hard time breastfeeding one, it wasn't going to be easier with two. I asked my mother to hold one of my breast towards baby A's mouth. Then I needed my husband to stand behind me so he could get a good grip on the other breast and lift it up for baby B to latch on. At the same time I was gently trying to cradle the heads of these two babies to manipulate them into, what they call a "football hold." (When I say "they" I mean the breastfeeding Nazis.) I just want these two little screaming infants to suck the skin off my ever so sensitive nipples at the same time so I can finally "sleep when they sleep." (Yes, another little saying I learned from the breastfeeding Nazis).

Meanwhile, my father's screaming out orders like, "Why don't you try to put his head at a 90 degree angle?" I don't think my husband ever fully recovered from being that close to my mother, my father, and my leaking breasts at the same time. #PassTheTitCream

I did the old college try and I breastfed the twins as long as I could. I remember one day I didn't even bother to put on a shirt at all. I never got them to feed at the same time, so I had to do it separately. It took me so long to feed one baby that by the time I was finished with this one, the other one was ready to eat again. By the way, those are the names of my twins – this one and the other one. I love those names.

All these years everyone's been telling me, including those breastfeeding Nazis, that breast feeding had all the vitamins and nutrients that you need and it's the best thing you can do for your baby. Well, fast forward to when I had my third child 5 years later they told me that I had to give my child vitamins if I was breastfeeding and I said, "Why?"

Well, we've found that breast milk doesn't have all the vitamins and nutrients that a baby needs. So when I stopped breastfeeding I didn't have to give my child any supplements and that the powdered milk I was giving him was all that he needed. So don't for a second feel guilty if you don't breastfeed. Don't for a second let any breastfeeding Nazis tell you what to do. Do what's right for you, your baby, and your family. Who gives a shit what the breastfeeding Nazis say or anyone else for that matter. Including your know-it-all friend, mother, or aunt. When they asked if you're breastfeeding in that condescending voice, just tell them in the nicest voice you can muster up, that you've decided to do what's best for your family. That your husband is the only one who's allowed to suck on your breast at this time. He's much gentler at it and he promises not to do it every 3 hours.

When we switched to bottle feeding I had to boil the water and prepare for eight feedings a day. Now, times that by two and you get sixteen bottles. Sixteen bottles a day every day for a long time. Those were the days when I wished I was a cat, nine nipples!

The feedings got a little easier when low and behold it was my very effective and efficient husband who discovered a much more efficient way to feed these little bundles of milk munchers. He would do a lot of the late night feedings when he got home from work. One night he put them both on the floor each in a Boppy nursing pillow carefully putting their heads close together. He then sat on the floor right in front of them, holding each of the bottles at the same time and feeding them at the same time! He even was able to hold both the bottles in one hand while he read the sports section. When I saw this I was amazed and mad that I – the mother of all mothers – didn't think of it. And a guy thought of it! How dare he!

The babies had fewer feeding times, they slept a little longer, and playtime was easier and so much more fun as they got older. So every month or so it changed and got a little different, but one thing remained the same – I always had to do everything twice. If you're doing it once, you might as well do it twice, said nobody ever! If you put one in that car seat, that takes a rocket scientist to figure out, you gotta put the other one in the other car seat. You feed one mashed up peas, you gotta feed the other one mashed up peas. You put one kid's shoes on, you gotta put the other kid's shoes on. That's four shoes. Thank you God, for inventing Velcro.

You tell one kid he's behaving nicely and before you can tell the other one he's behaving nicely all of a sudden he starts behaving even better to get a compliment, too. Hmm, this is ingenious! Instead of being a real *Mean Mommy* and saying, "Why can't you be more like your brother?" all I have to do is just reward the correct behavior and the other one does better! I'm getting to like this twin thing! Look how easy that was. This little experiment works every time and still does to this day!

I had them together all the time. They slept together in the small bassinet. Then they slept together in the same crib for a long time. Then I separated them into their own cribs as they got bigger and more rambunctious. I think I had more abandonment issues then they did when I separated them. The same thing happened when I just recently separated them into their own rooms for the first time ever in thirteen years. They didn't seem to mind meanwhile I felt like a washed up sea lion waiting for her babies to come back home. I was lucky my boys, for the most part, were very good and easy babies. I had little bit to do with it of course, but they were always very content with each other and they didn't need me much at all. Even now into their teenage years they're still very close. They entertain each other, they have each other's back, they take care of each other, and still to this day they're on the same poop schedule. #thankgodfor2bathrooms

There were some days that having twins wasn't so easy. Like when they were little and they both wanted me at the same time. Those were some rough days. I had to get in our big recliner chair, lean back and let them crawl on top of me and cry. Oh God, I was in agony back then thinking about all the stuff I had to do, trying to rock the twins and get them to stop crying. One of them would finally settle down and then there was one. That one, never settled down. Nothing seemed to work, except the swing. One night I even said, "Why can't you be more like your brother?" But that didn't even work. He had to sleep in the swing for the whole night. As soon as you shut it off the crying would begin. Needless to say the motor burnt out and we had to get another one. Three swings later and he was still crying.

My favorite thing in the world was bath time with the twins. I had them both in the bath at the same time sitting in their little bath rings, so they don't fall over, facing each other.

With all their toys, floats and boats. The best part was the little squirt gun. Now nailing these little, milk nibblers with squirt guns was by far the best therapy I've ever had. After bath time, it was even more fun. I would lather them up in that baby lavender cream that made them smell so good you could just eat them. Then they would love to run around and chase each other naked. For some reason this made them laugh their little cellulite tushes off. They would run and chase each other then hug each other. This was truly my favorite time of the day and some of my most fond memories of the twins. That being said, this was also one of the scariest times I've ever had being a mom.

One night at bath time, the twins just turned one-year-old and they were doing their little thing chasing each other naked, laughing and hugging. Then Cameron hugged Harry so hard he knocked him down and he landed back on his head and he just lay there. He didn't get up. He was passed out for about 45 seconds and that was the scariest and longest 45 seconds of my life. I ran to get the phone to call 911 at the same time I was holding him trying to wake him up. He was just stiff. In my panic state, I dialed 411 and before I could hang up and try again he woke up. Then the tears ran down my face just as hard and fast as I hugged and kiss my baby. I think my heart stopped for 45 seconds that night.

Looking back at this moment I was thinking to myself, "411! Really?" I'd like to think that I would be calm, cool and collected at a time like that. I can't even dial 911 right. Really what would I do if they answered? "411, can I help you?" "Can you give me the number for an emergency?!" I don't think I ever told anyone I did that. I was too embarrassed, now I'm telling the world. I almost couldn't save my child because I dialed 411 instead. You never know what you're going to do in an emergency situation. I hope I do better the next time. What am I saying! I hope there's not a next time. Anyway, I was alone when this happened; my husband was on the road. Luckily my neighbor was a nurse and her mother baby-sits for our children. So they came right over to help. I got right in the emergency room and they double checked everything and, after all kinds of tests, it turns out he just got his "bells rung" so they say.

Side note: anytime you have to go to the emergency room go with a nurse. They rule! I'm so lucky nothing bad happened and I thank the good lord for that. Having babies is so hard anything can go wrong at any time. That's the most stressful part about being a parent. They're so precious. I thank God every day for having healthy babies and I know how lucky I am. I never take that for granted, not even for a second or 45 seconds. I've never gone from such happiness to such panic to such happiness again in my whole life. I would never, ever want to go through that again. I would however, like to see them chase each other naked again. Not now, they're a little older so that would be weird, but if I could turn back time I would turn it back to bath time with the twins, in a heartbeat.

MEAN MOMMY ON BITING

Every child's different and every parent is different so what works for you may not work for me. You have to know and trust your instincts in situations when you're working on correcting your own child's behavior.

One of my twins was biting his brother all the time. He was not biting me or other children, thank God. He would just bite his brother. Which was good because his brother deserved it. Just kidding, but he was the evil twin. Nonetheless, he was very young at the time and I kept on giving him time outs. I was always saying no and taking away his toys. Anything I could do to make him understand that this was not appropriate behavior. This was difficult because he was so young and he didn't understand what exactly he was doing and he couldn't explain his frustration.

Well, one day he was in his time out for biting the evil one (I mean baby B) for the umpteenth time and this time he actually broke the skin. I was so fed up with his behavior. As I was looking at this poor little boy in his time out, I could just tell he had no idea what he was doing and the pain he was causing the evil one (I did it again, baby B). He just didn't understand why I was getting so mad. So I trusted my instincts, as a mother, walked over into the corner, got down on my knees, looked him right in the eyes and said, "Do you know what a bite feels like? Do you know what you're doing to your brother? Do you know why he's crying? This is what a bite feels like. This is what you do to your brother."

I took his little finger and very gently, yet firmly bit his finger until he said, "Ouch!"

And I said, "That's what it feels like. Now you sit there and think about that." Well, I guess he did because, as God as my witness, from that day on he never bit his brother again. Not even once. He's still hitting him, kicking him, and he pulls out his hair, but that's beside the point.

I knew it was going to work, but I didn't think it would work that well. I'm so glad I trusted myself and did what everyone tells you not to do. I'm so glad I decided to try it. God forbid as mothers we trust our natural born instincts to actually take care of our own children, but rather go by what all the books and all the so-called experts tell you to do. I'm thankful I was smart enough to trust my own instincts as a mother! I'm so thankful I was a *Mean Mommy* to my son that day.

NIGHT TIME DAY CARE

My twins were about three-years-old and I took a gig that was for a whole week in Atlantic City, N.J. at the Borgata. I lost a lot of work after having kids because I could never be away for that long without my kids. This gig was a little different: I could drive to it, it was in a really nice hotel, and I only had to do fifteen minutes a night. The rest of the time I could be by the pool with the kids, take them to the movies, the park, the boardwalk, Chuck E. Cheese, and have a blast.

I got the gig in plenty of time to get a babysitter all lined up. When you're at a casino, the babysitting agencies mark up the price so high, they make you do a minimum of four hours, and they add on all these convenience fees. That's worse than losing all your money at the craps table. I remember I paid a babysitter 300 bucks (not including the tip) so I could do Last Comic Standing at the Paris Hotel in Vegas! That was a "fine how do ya do" right after losing on national TV. So for this gig, I didn't want to lose money so I researched all my options.

After much research, I finally settled on an agency and I negotiated a good price. I had promised her two hours every night for a week. I only needed 15 minutes, but I figured I would go to the nice gym they had at the hotel, shower in the spa take my time getting ready, do the show and come back to the room. I'm always trying to get ready for my show by putting on make-up with one hand while feeding a baby in the other. So this will be a nice little break for me. I made sure to call and confirm a week in advance. I'm never this organized, but when it comes to mixing kids with work you have to be.

I called the morning of my gig and that's when things got a little messed up. She tells me she's getting someone. I kept my cool as much as I could and I said I had this booked for months, I called a week ago to confirm, you already have my paperwork and now you're telling me you don't have anyone? I will be down there early in the afternoon and I will call you then. She assured me she was working on it and there will be someone there. I checked into the hotel early.

Our room is very nice with plenty of room for the three of us. It was about four hours until my gig and the woman had called me back to tell me she's finally got someone and that she couldn't come early, but she would be there in time for me to make it to my gig. Thank God, I could breathe easy now. I took the kids on a tour and showed them the big theater I was working in that night. I took them back stage and I checked in with the people who were working back there.

The kids thought that was so cool... and that was the last time I smiled that whole day.

I was ready for my gig. The twins were already nestled in their Pack-n-Play that was in the bathroom and they were just about to fall asleep. All the baby-sitter had to do was sit in the room watch anything she wanted on the TV for a little over fifteen minutes. I could not have made it any easier.

The phone rang, it was the booker, "Kerri, where are you?" "I'm right upstairs and I'm just waiting for the sitter who will be here soon. I'm coming." Panic set in. I'll never work this gig again. Where the fuck is that babysitter? I called the agency and they were not there. I called the front desk to ask if they'd seen her and told them to call me as soon as they did. I was just about to gather my little ones and bring them to the show when finally the front desk called. I ran out into the hallway to meet her I had no more time to spare. I told her three things, "The boys are in their bed just about to go to sleep. Please just sit and watch TV quietly. I will be back in 15 minutes."

Just looking at her for the few seconds I had in the hallway of the hotel, I noticed two teeth missing, ripped jeans, smoke on her breath, and glassy eyes. I ran downstairs in tears thinking I had just left my children with a crack addict. As I ran into the elevator I heard my room telephone ringing again. Oh my God, I will never work here again. I'd better be fucking funny tonight! He will never use me as a comic again. I'm not reliable, I'm a woman, I have kids, I'm not funny, all that shit was in my head. Not to mention, my kids may not be there when I get back all because Mommy wants a career! I'm the worst mommy ever.

My only saving grace is that there were cameras everywhere and you had to show the guard your room key to get up into the room elevators. I kept telling myself that to calm me down. I kept telling myself, that I'm doing the right thing and that I'm a good mom as I ran past the guard yelling at him, "Stop any woman leaving with two little boys. I will be back in 15 minutes!"

To this day this was one of the most gut wrenching feelings of motherhood I had ever experienced. I ran backstage. I wiped away my tears as they said my name, took a deep breath, and walked out to a live audience. I don't remember a thing after that. To this day this was one of the weirdest fifteen minutes I have ever done in my life. I've never just put my act on auto pilot before like that. I don't even remember telling a joke. I had no idea if any of my jokes got laughs and I didn't care. All I needed to do was to get back up to my twins. I got back and I saw that my twins were not sleeping. They were jumping up and down on the hotel beds and watching a movie, which ended up costing me more than what I paid the babysitter. I didn't care as long as they were all right and as long as I was not in the headlines the next day: *Mother lets a crack addict watch her twins while she goes out gambling!*

I said three things to her: "Thank you very much. Here's your money. You and your agency are fired."

The next day I was on a mission to find a new agency and a new sitter. It took me a whole day to find something or someone and the only thing I could find was a situation that was not much better than what I had. It was exactly like a day care, but it was at night. I took a tour of the place and talked with the owner and paid to take my kids there for two hours every night. Not the best scenario, but it would do for now.

We got into a nice routine. We had so much fun all day. The kids loved the pool – we were in it for hours. I'm a swim instructor so basically they learned everything about swimming that whole week. We went to lunch in all the coolest places – Chuck E. Cheese being the coolest. Then we went to the day care to play with our new friends. My boys were the only white kids in the day care and that was normal to them. We still lived in Harlem, so it was just like their day care at home. For years my kids thought they were the minority. I would drop them off go to the gym, do my show, and then pick them up.

One day my brother called and said he was in town for business and he had time to take me out to eat and go to my show. What fun, an unexpected visitor. I remember not feeling well that night and not doing much of the talking. My brother didn't notice anything because he talks a lot. We had a nice dinner at one of the casino's steak houses. He watched my show, and came with me to pick up my kids. He was in complete awe of what had happened with the babysitter and what I was doing all week with the kids. He quietly said to me. "Kerri, you're so brave." He didn't mean it in a good way like, I could fight off a grizzly bear or anything like that. He meant it, like I'm not so sure I would do this.

I still for some reason wasn't feeling well and I just wanted to lie down, but he still kept talking until all of a sudden out of nowhere, I grabbed the ice bucket and started violently throwing up. I hurled so loudly, the twins started laughing. Mommy what is that? Mommy what's that funny sound? I would have laughed too if I wasn't trying to figure out what the hell was happening to me. They were laughing so hard you would have thought they were watching a YouTube video's of some funny monkeys eating their poo or something. My brother had no idea what to do. Should he help me, help the twins, get a new bucket or laugh? He was running around getting me towels, and trying to explain to the little guys that mommy's making all those weird noises because mommy is not feeling well, so you can stop laughing. All while trying not to laugh himself.

Finally I stopped and was able to get a hold of myself. My brother asked me if I wanted him to stay and I said, "No don't worry, it was probably something I ate. I will be fine. I got this." He did the best he could do to get me all I needed and get the kids settled back down, and he left.

All that night and the next morning I had the shivers, and I started to develop this rash all over my body. I mean all over my body between my legs, under my knees, under my armpits, back of my neck, under my chest, between my unmentionables. Everywhere! It was puffy, red, and it hurt. My stomach was so sore from throwing up and I had all these aches and pains. I had no idea what just happened to me and whatever it was, I had to pull it together to take care of my kids and be funny later that night. I figured I must have eaten something that was bad or had developed and allergy to something. I felt better as the day went on and was able to recover by the time my show started.

When we got home from the gig and I spent the rest of the week trying to figure out what happened and why I got so sick. I went to a few doctors and I had every test to every allergy you can imagine and everything came up negative. Fast forward to a few years later and I figured out that every time I got that same rash I was swimming with my boys. Turns out I'm allergic to bromine which is a form of chlorine. Bromine is known to be used by big hotels and pools where there's a lot of traffic because it's a stronger chemical. Looking back now I was swimming with my boys for hours for three days straight. No wonder I was violently ill. Now every time I'm about to go swimming, I have to ask the lifeguard what kind of chlorine they use. That was by far the worst time I've ever had on a gig. To this day my twins, who still don't know that I almost left them with a crack addict, say to me, "When are we going back to Atlantic City? That was one of the best vacations."

HELLO PRIVACY, ARE YOU THERE?

A s soon as you enter into the delivery room to experience the miracle of child birth for the first time, your privacy and dignity will go right out the window simultaneously, never to be returned. The pain you feel during that delivery is so intense that you don't even care what you look like, what you sound like, or how many people are starring at your swollen, stretched out, vagina. (Yes, I said it.) You won't even care about the fact that you think you might have to pass gas and/or do the unthinkable. Yes, you know what I'm talking about. Leaving a stool sample for the doctor when it's not required. Like I said in previous chapters, no one tells you about this little slice of heaven, not even your friends. It happens and it will happen to you, but you don't care, you just want that baby out of you. This little heartfelt moment, we call delivery, was designed to help you get over any reservation or shyness you may have had B.C. (before children). Privacy doesn't exist during parenting. Oh sure, you can try to find it, as you try breastfeeding, showering, or going to the bathroom. But it won't be there. You may even find it when you go for a car ride but then you have your phone, so you put it on silent, then you see the text message piling up. You try to find privacy in your closet, but somehow, some way they find you. Whatever you do, wherever you go, they will find you. They should've hired my kids to go find Osama bin Laden. It would've taken them minutes to find him. Plus all the screaming would've irritated him way more than water boarding or any other torture – he would have given up all his secrets immediately.

MEAN MOMMY ON POTTY TRAINING

How come when your toddler finally goes poop in the toilet you go crazy? You tell everyone, you invite everyone to see it, your family, your neighbors, and your cat. You end up having a big, huge, potty poop parade. But if your husband does it, it's rude, disgusting and you have to evacuate the premises.

VAGINA FITNESS

With two boys at home I wanted to try for a baby girl. I wanted a little girl so badly. I really didn't care about the sexes of my twins. It was my first pregnancy. Obviously my main concern and the most important thing was that they were...black. I'm kidding, but did you ever see a newborn black baby – it's so cute. You must admit a newborn white baby looks like a wrinkled old man. Asian babies look so cute, too. Did you ever see an Asian baby coming out of the womb with her hair sticking straight up like a troll doll at the end of a pencil? Oh my God, so cute, right? I really wanted a black baby and an Asian baby for twins. *Not only would I look like Angelina Jolie, I would have a good chance for a sports or math scholarship.*

I realized I wanted a girl the second I gave birth to my boys. I was so happy I had two boys, but as soon as I gave birth all I wanted was my MOM. She was the only one who would make this huge momentous yet scariest time of my life better. Who better than my mom to help me though motherhood. That's when I knew I needed a little girl to grow up, have a baby and want to be by my side. More than any place in the world I wanted to be by my mother's side after giving birth. These boys are going to grow up and move out and be with their mothers-in-law. I can't let that happen. I need to bring a little girl in this world, so I bought a book on how to have a baby girl. I learned that I could eat certain foods that would help produce a girl. I learned that different sexual positions would help in getting the baby girl of my dreams. I showed the book to my husband and he got excited, pointed to one of the pictures in the book and said, "I want to have sex this way! This way will get us the baby girl!" I looked at it and said, "Honey, that way will produce NO baby at all." So we got pregnant again and I was so excited, but I still wasn't going to find out. I wanted to wait. I wanted to be surprised. I was too scared to find out. Sure enough just as we carefully planned it out – it was a boy!

People would look at me walking around pregnant with two boys and say such things like, "Hope it's a girl." Or "Are you trying for the girl now?" I hated everyone forcing their opinions onto me. Do you know what it is? Are you going to find out? Are you praying for the girl? This is exactly why I didn't want to know the sex. Every time some idiot stranger would say something like that I would have to be reminded that, "No, God didn't answer my prayers he hates me, thanks for reminding me of that, and I now can be depressed for three more months until the baby's born." So to screw with these people the next time anyone asked me, "Do you know what the sex is?" I would say, "What the sex is? I don't even know who the father is!" or "No, I don't know the sex, but we're hoping it's a boy who identifies with being a girl."

Don't worry about me – I'm all right with three boys. Let's be honest, if I gave birth to a little girl, I'd be jealous that she would be skinner and prettier than me and then I would have to get rid of her. That's a joke – I would never get rid of her, I would sell her on eBay. Don't worry I love this child. He's my favorite one. I mean, he's my youngest one. I don't have a favorite, I love all my children equally, but if they all ran into the street at the same time I would chase after that one first. Because he's the youngest. I'm done having children and for a second, I thought I might want one more, but then I remembered that I was self-centered. Tell no one this or it will ruin me, and I will no longer have an excuse as to why I'm incompetent, but twins are much easier. At least in my case they were. They had each other so they for the most part were content and didn't need me. So, I secretly wanted twins again. If I was going to have another baby I was going to do it right away so I would have them close in age and possibly have Irish twins. When it really came down to making the decision of having another child, I chickened out.

All I kept thinking was that I would have twins again and it would be boys again, and then I would basically have giving birth to 5 boys. That would mean I would have a basketball team in my house and the owner of the team doesn't make enough money to pay them all. Naturally, my husband got snipped the very next day. However, he never went for his final checkup to see if it worked. So now, I'm always left wondering, every month, if I'm pregnant or if I'm just getting fat. Secret is...I wouldn't mind a teeny, tiny, cute little mistake.

I wanted to know what it was like to have a baby the way you're supposed to have it, the old fashioned way, through the birth canal! To really experience the meaning of life and to see the true blessings of the miracle of birth! So for my second pregnancy, third child I was going to give birth through the birth canal, in the corn fields, while I'm husking the corn. Once you've had a C-section and you decide to have a birth canal birth, they call that a V-back. They should call it "you're an idiot doing it this way-back"! No one told me I wouldn't be able to sneeze, laugh or do jumping jacks without peeing all over myself for the rest of my life! What the hell was I thinking? I was already scarred from the first C-section why the hell would I want to do a v-back. Now I'm scarred both ways.

But no one tells you the bad things! I will. If you're at all thinking maybe I should see what it's like to have a natural birth. Stop those feelings right now. A few years later no one is ever going to care how that thing came out of you. Years from now, no one is going ask you how that thing came out of you. Even that thing isn't going to care how it came out of you and neither will you. All you will be left with is memories of you painfully trying to push something big out your holier-than-thou birth canal while unbeknownst to you shitting in a bed pan. YES, involuntarily shitting. No one tells you that and yes you will. Hopefully the nurses and your husband or partner will keep that on the down low. (No pun intended.) Now I will ask you again, is that worth a reminder that every time you sneeze, laugh, or cough you will pee your pants?

NO, it's not worth it! Especially if you're already scarred up! So when you're thinking of your birth plan think of me. Well don't think of me, that would be weird, but think of this little story I'm about to tell you.

Not only am I a standup comic, but I'm also a personal trainer and aerobics instructor. While trying to get hired at this new gym in town, I had to take this young girl's kickboxing class because I was being auditioned to take over the class. All of a sudden she screams out, "OK EVERYBODY DO

JUMPING JACKS FOR A MINUTE!" Now I didn't want her to think I was out of shape and I couldn't do jumping jacks for a minute and not get the job.

Of course, I could do it. I was in shape for chrissake. I could do jumping jacks for 10 minutes, but not without peeing all over myself. Luckily I was wearing black yoga pants and I had a jacket to tie around my waist so when she told me to have a seat in her office after class to discuss future job opportunities I was all set. I got the job and immediately changed that part to "EVERYBODY DO LOW IMPACT KICKS FOR A MINUTE!"

There's an operation to fix this. Which I'm looking into! Forget those Kegel exercises they tell you to do, they don't work. Well, they do a little but you have to do them 24/7. Believe me, I have better things to do than to squeeze my vagina and hold for 10 seconds. They also told me that besides the operation I could first try to solve the problem by doing the Kegels while using a tool. Tools? You want me to stick tools up there? I don't think so. If I'm not doing it for my husband then I'm not doing it for you. I'll take the in/out operation please! (The in/out pun was indeed intended there.)

Do you know what rich celebrities do in Hollywood? They schedule a C-section with their OBGYN and their plastic surgeon two weeks before their baby's due date so their stomach doesn't get too stretched out. They give birth to a perfect baby with the perfect round head, and then their plastic surgeon takes the time to give them a tight, mini tummy tuck. They sew them back up nice and neat that won't create scar tissue or give them a huge ugly scar!

That's why they look so good two days after birth! That's why you see them in a bikini two minutes after birth, vacationing in

Bali and doing jumping jacks on the beach! You can't compare yourself to another celebrity who is pregnant the same time you are. They have the staff, the money, and the means to make giving birth look like an all day spa excursion and God bless them, Bitches! #KimKardasianDoesJumpingJacksForAMinute

MEAN MOMMY ON TEMPER TANTRUMS, FRUSTRATIONS AND MELTDOWNS

Not yours, but your kids. One way to help with your child being frustrated is to teach them sign language as early as four months. That way you don't have to talk to them before you've had your morning coffee.

The more they sleep the less they have breakdowns. Get your child to sleep on time! If you think your children are running around like crazy because they have all this energy and they're not tired, think again, that's exactly what they are – TIRED! Put them to BED! Believe it or not eating healthy, drinking water, less snacking will help with these breakdowns. You can't reason with a crazy person so if you find that your lectures aren't working, forget about it and put him to bed, time out, or quiet time and talk about it later. He's too tired to comprehend anything so drop it for another time.

Once my son was hysterically crying, "Mommy, I said a BAD word and I don't want you to get mad at me!" Being the good mother that I am, I said. "Oh baby, I won't get mad at you what did you say?"

"I can't tell you."

"Oh you can tell me. What does it start with?"

"B," he said.

Well, let me tell you that I went through every swear word that starts with a "B" until finally I realize this kid doesn't know what the hell he's talking about and he should just go to bed. I can't believe I let this go one for more than one minute especially when it was at bedtime. I know better than to try to reason with a kid who is clearly drunk from his own exhaustion. He had no idea what he said and he couldn't even remember when he said it and now he knows every swear word in the dictionary that starts with "B", thanks to his very own mom. I can hear the kindergarten teacher now. "Hi, Mrs. Cotter. Your son said 'Boobies, Bastard, Boogies, Balls, Butt, and Beaver' and then he called me a 'Bitch.'"

THERE'S NO CRYING IN COMEDY

Remember when I said I will never move eight months pregnant again? Well I kept my promise, I never moved eight months pregnant – I moved nine months pregnant.

We decided to move to the suburbs. We found our dream house with great schools and it was on a cul-de-sac! The only problem was it wasn't ready to move in until the end of July. My due date was August 1st and we had already sold our apartment and had to move out in June. So I planned to work and live at my parent's small beach shack in Cape Cod until we could move in.

We planned my doctor's visit the day we had to be in the city for the closing and this was the day that screwed up all that nice planning. The closing was fine, but the gynecologist visit took a whole new turn. I remember the doctor looked at me while she was feeling around up there and said so if you want your baby to be born in Boston you're free to go, but if you...and just then I felt this intense pressure as if a fist was going up my ho-ho and into my intestine...want the baby to be delivered here in New York you need to stay here, because you're probably going to have the baby soon. I have three weeks left, and I still have all my stuff, all my kids and my weekend gigs up in Massachusetts. "Well, are there good doctors where you are?" she asked.

No. Oh my God what am I going to do? I'm homeless, nine months pregnant, taking care of 4-year-old twin boys. I didn't care what she said, I had a feeling I wasn't close to having this baby. If anything I feel like I'm going to go PAST my due date. I want to go back up to Massachusetts to work and be with my family. Then that night I felt such pain in my abdomen and I got scared I called my cousin and she said, "Oh yeah, you got fisted by your gynecologist!" What?! "They do that sometimes when they want the baby to come out. They go up there and try to break your mucus plug." She said it happened to her and it's painful. She said her doctor wanted to help things move along up there so she put her fist and did something with her fingers to try to break her mucus plug. Doctors have their own agendas and it's all about being there when you're ready to go so they get the paycheck before they go on vacation! So I got scared and thought she was right I'm going to have the baby right now. I have to get all my things, get my children, cancel all my gigs and find a place to live. I was in my car because I had no other place to go, and I started to call all the bookers to cancel my gigs.

At first I had a professional voice and then out of nowhere I started to cry while I was on the phone with one of the bookers. This was one of the saddest times of my career. First of all bookers of almost all comedy clubs hate dealing with women, not to mention women's issues! This is by far the biggest women's issue ever. It took months of back and forth phone calls, emails, sending him links to my shows, doing free shows for him to prove to him I can do the job for him to finally trust me to even do this gig in the first place and now I'm canceling on him. I worked so hard to get those gigs and begged for them and now I'm canceling them.

I hate the fact that you always have to prove yourself, that you're just as good as a guy if not better all the time and here I am not only canceling a gig, but sobbing to him like a girl. I was crying because I didn't want him to know that I'm a woman having a baby! I think the tears gave it away. Oh God, I kept telling myself, he will never book me again. I hated that moment. I hated everything about it. I hated that I tried so hard to cover the fact that I was a real woman with real woman problems and that I started to cry. #theresnocryingincomedy

There's no crying in comedy! I hated the fact that he would have no sympathy for me for doing something so wonderful by bringing the miracle of life into this world. Fuck him for making me feel that way. Fuck me for letting him make me feel that way. I'm mad that I'm a woman for the very same reason I'm so proud to be a woman. All these mixed feelings came into play for what? For a shitty gig in the basement of a shit hole of a place. That only 4 people, 8 drunks and 1 asshole will go to. So I lost that gig for life. But gained the best thing in my life, another life!

So after all that... the baby came on his due date! I could have been the Super Woman, the super comic, the super mom and I could have done it all, but because my doctor had other plans I cancelled all those gigs, made my mother pack all my crap all two of my kids' crap and bring them to me. We all had to sleep on a piece of plywood because the rugs didn't show up on time. Here I am nine months pregnant sleeping on plywood waiting for rugs and a baby. So I ask again how does that saying go? We plan, and God laughs!

MEAN MOMMY ON
BATHROOM ETIQUETTE

As soon as I shut the door to go to the bathroom, all hell breaks loose. All three kids suddenly need me at once! Last time I went to the bathroom, I locked the door. They were pounding on it, yelling, "Mom, what are you doing?"

"I'll be right out!" I shouted, as I started opening the tampon wrapper.

Then one of the twins screamed, "MOM, WHAT'S THAT NOISE?...DO YOU HAVE CANDY IN THERE?"

GET THE BUCKET HE'S
THROWING UP! AGAIN!

When one gets sick they all get sick. They always seem to get sick at the most inopportune times? There's never a good time for your kids to get sick, but there is a worst time to get sick – and my kids always pick the worst time to get sick. It's always when I'm away, or when I'm about to go away, or he's away, we're all away, or in the car. My son Harrison would throw up a lot. For one thing he would get car sick. He was also allergic to egg whites and cashew nuts, but he would get car sick all the time and throw up, and I didn't discover that he was allergic to this stuff until he was four-years-old. Can you imagine? For four years I had been giving my kid egg whites and never knew he had an allergy to it. Everything has eggs in it. Everything. I just thought he was a whiny kid that got car sick. I'm such a bad mommy! Looking back now I remember each time he got sick and I just thought it was something else. Never a food allergy. He's created quite the scene at Wal-Mart when he threw up out of nowhere all over the cart, the food we were buying, and the floor. The poor woman working there saw it and then SHE threw up all over the place. Loud speakers came on, alarms went off. We had just gotten there so again, I thought it was the car ride.

There was this industry party at the Comic Strip in New York City for families, managers, agents and such. I remember having to get up and leave because my son was so whiny. I was embarrassed so I hailed a cab and left. He threw up in the cab. I didn't know if he was sick, car sick, or just hated the industry folks like I did. Looking back now, he must have eaten something with eggs or cashews at the party.

When the twins were two and I was in Vegas doing *Last Comic Standing* – we had to bring the kids with us because my husband Tom was in the competition, too. My mother and father came to help babysit and show their support, so we figured we could make it work. I gave Harry some eggs that had salmon in them at the buffet at the Paris hotel. Twenty minutes later he threw up right in the lobby of this gorgeous hotel, all over himself and his stroller. Thank God it was early enough for me to clean it up and get ready for the BIGGEST NIGHT OF MY LIFE and be on NATIONAL TV. I had to get my game face on so I didn't think too much of it. I just thought the salmon must have gone bad. Later after losing the competition we drove from Vegas to L.A. and he threw up in the car. *FYI I did go further than my very funny, famous husband did on *Last Comic Standing*! I know it was because I had bigger boobs then he did, but I'm going with, it was because I was funnier than he was. #LastSpouseStanding

Fast forward to a year later when a producer saw both Tom and me on *Last Comic Standing* and thought that we would make a great reality show. We signed a deal with WE

Entertainment to film 6 episodes called *Two Funny,* a show about two comics and their twins on the road to stardom. We decided to do the first filming at the most prestigious comedy festival in the industry, the Montreal Just For Laughs Festival. Tom had a show in upstate New York the night before so we decided that he would drive the minivan with all our stuff and I would fly alone with the twins to the festival in Canada. What could go wrong? It was only a one hour flight!

When we got to Canada, the shuttle came to pick all the comics, managers, agents, and VIP's and bring us to the hotel. There I was with twins trying to make a good impression – like yes, I'm the star of my new reality show, look at me I'm at the Montreal Comedy Festival. It's hard to look like a movie star, when you're trying to get in a van filled with industry who are waiting for you to collapse a double stroller, gather your diaper bag and get your two, 2-year-old boys buckled in. So we're about a mile away from our hotel and Harry gets car sick and throws up all over me, all over the van and on the manager I was trying to impress. I wanted to just die as I sat there with vomit all over me and the real Hollywood movie stars in the back gagging over the smell. Where were the cameras for my reality show then? That's some good entertainment right there. Maybe if they filmed that little scene, our show would still be on the air.

I finally got to the hotel. I quickly got all of our clothes off and into the tub to clean everybody. Not realizing that my husband who was supposed to meet me at the hotel with all of our clothes and luggage was going to be three hours late. So here I am naked with twin boys with nothing but a diaper on waiting for daddy to come to our hotel on the SECOND BIGGEST NIGHT OF MY CAREER. Do you think God was telling me to quit comedy? An industry party, the two biggest nights of my career and I had to deal with a sick kid? I didn't see the signs because I was trying too hard.

My son Harry has thrown up so much that I now have it down to a science. I've started collecting those throw up bags you get on the plane and I've stashed them in every corner of my house, car, his book bag, and my pocketbook. I couldn't understand how he could go on every single roller coaster ride, turning him upside down and inside out and not even throw up. He would even ride these crazy rides right after he ate a whole double bacon cheeseburger and nothing. Yet two seconds in a car and everything he's eaten since pre-school comes out of his mouth.

I was eight months pregnant and my husband goes on the road for a few days and he's going to meet us in Florida where we plan to go visit our parents during the twins' pre-school vacation. We were selling our apartment in Harlem at the time so I thought that with the kids out of the house for a week, that the house would be clean and a good time to have an open house during the week we're away. So now not only do I have to pack for me and the twins, I have to make sure the house is completely spotless before I leave in preparation for the open house. Already this is a lot of pressure on a pregnant woman. The night was going smoothly. I had just sweated my ass off cleaning the house and I had just finished packing for the boys. I knew it was going take me a long time to pack because I had no idea if I was going to fit into anything now that I'm 8 months pregnant. I wanted to quickly get it done so I could go to bed early because I had to do a call in radio show early the next morning. So while I'm trying on some things my son decides to throw up all over the bathroom floor. Believe it or not it wasn't

Harry. It was Cameron this time. The poor kid was sick. Yes, he threw up all over the bathroom that I had just cleaned spotless.

Did you have any idea that throw up can stain bathroom tile? Well it can and it did. My son stained the black tile in the bathroom making it look like a murder had just happened. Instead of packing to fly to Florida, I'm up all night taking care of my sick boy, knowing I'll be doing this all over again in three days with his twin brother and hoping I will be able to do it in sunny Florida. Praying that the hotel doesn't have black tiles in their bathrooms. So in between throw ups, I'm trying to figure out how I will be able to get up by 6 AM and be alert for my radio talk show. Plus I had to call the super to see if he could get the tile fixed, finish packing for three kids, get the throw up smell out of my house, and make it to my flight by 2 PM. All while leaving my home to complete strangers to walk through and judge my interior design decisions. Hoping that they don't walk into the bathroom and think that someone had just died in there. I learned one thing during this whole fiasco. I could never kill my husband and get away with it. I cleaned for hours and still left evidence. I'm still 8 months pregnant and I'm about to snap. So I was up half the night helping my son who threw up every 1/2 hour, while trying to pack summer clothes that could fit a pregnant woman. I've come up with nothing. I've decided to just roll up my jeans and sleeves and wear the same old maternity crap I've been wearing this whole winter, and forget about swimming. I remember thinking before my head hit the pillow that all I have to do is my radio show in the morning, call the super to fix the bathroom tile before the open house, and pack a few more things. I'll keep the house and the kids clean until we have to go. I'll get the doorman to help me in the cab with all my luggage and the double stroller. I will do curb side check-in at the airport. Easy Peasy. Then I can relax in sunny Florida. Then I prayed that my son gets better and that his twin, for the love of God doesn't get it. Knowing that if he does get sick he is, by now, a true professional at throwing up in public.

It seemed like the alarm went off before I even finished saying my prayers. "Did I even sleep last night?" I asked myself. I'm so tired, but the good news is that my kids were still asleep. The bad news is that five minutes before I'm about to go on the radio I see a crew outside my office window ready to cut the bricks off the side of my apartment with some kind of loud obnoxious jack hammer.

I panicked and kept banging on the window trying to explain to the workers that they cannot start hammering until I'm done. I kept holding up my hands in a cross and then showing 7 fingers to say NO MORE FOR 7 MINUTES. They had to hold off work for at least 7 minutes. Which is how long my air time was for that segment. I know it doesn't seem like a lot but in radio it's a lot and I was proud to have my seven minutes to tell the world, all right, the 79 listeners my jokes. They just looked at me like I was some crazy pregnant lady, because...I was exactly that. I don't think they understood what I was saying, but they knew not to get in the way of some pregnant bitch so they stopped. Now, all I had to do was be funny on the radio. This is very hard for a comic to do at 6 in the morning, especially after the night I just had and the fiasco in the morning. The second I was done with my interview the jack hammer started and the kids woke up screaming. Then within a half hour dust had filled my whole apartment leaving a layer of ugly, brown film all over the shelves I dusted, and on just about everything else in the house, after I just spent my whole night cleaning.

That's when I broke down and lost it! I ran into the bathroom shut the door and called my husband screaming into his voicemail like a complete lunatic. OUR BATHROOM FLOOR IS STAINED, OUR WHOLE APARTMENT LOOKS LIKE DESERT STORM, OUR SON IS SICK, THE OTHER ONE IS PROBABLY ABOUT TO HURL, I HAVE TO LEAVE FOR THE AIRPORT IN 3 HOURS WITH THE APARTMENT COMPLETELY CLEAN FOR THE OPEN HOUSE, I'M NOT EVEN FINISHED PACKING YET, I HAVE NOTHING TO WEAR, AND I'M FAT!! NOT BECAUSE I'M PREGNANT, I'M JUST FAT!! With that same tone I hung up and called the super, a cleaning service, and a therapist. Problem solved.

MEAN MOMMY ON SICK KIDS

What is it about your bed that makes your kids feel better? I know that every once in a while it's okay to have your child sleep in your bed when they're sick, but here's how I feel and you're probably not going to like it because it's **mean**. Your kids need to learn how to be sick on their own, and sleep in their own beds when they're sick You need to teach them how to get up out of their beds and aim for the toilet or get the bucket. Don't baby a sick child. Yes, love them with all your might and rub their backs while they throw up, you can even get a cold face cloth to put on the back of their necks, but don't turn it into a three-ring circus. Otherwise you're going to get a call in the middle of the night when your child's in his twenties, drunk and throwing up asking you if he can come over and sleep with you and Daddy. (P.S. He may just ask to bring his girlfriend along...or boyfriend.)

THE MOTHER OF ALL VACATIONS

This was going to be the vacation of a lifetime! Daddy was working on a cruise the four days before Christmas and we all got invited to go. We were to fly out of the country and stay on some remote island at this luxurious and elegant resort to board the cruise the next day. The cruise was going to have so many fun things for the kids to do; I thought I would really be able to relax on this vacation. The kids were so excited.

I was excited too, but I knew my work was cut out for me, because we were getting back the night before Christmas. I had to get every gift bought, wrapped, and hidden before we left. I had to get all our summer clothes out, packed and ready to go. When I told the kids that we had to miss school on Friday to go on the cruise, I thought I was going to get an award for Mother of the Year. Instead I got a little 7-year-old crying and whining that he's going to miss "Pajama Day."

"I'm going to miss pajama day all for this stupid cruise!" The twins laughed, which made it worse. We tried to explain to the little guy that the cruise was going to be for 4 whole days of fun, instead of one day in your PJ's at school. But he was not buying it. I thought we finally settled that mess and not a day later he started saying he couldn't see. He got so much attention from the twins trying to give him an eye test by holding up signs with letters on them and continuously asking how many fingers they had up. Next thing you know, I'm at the doctor's office testing his eyes. He just had a physical and passed the eye test with flying colors! Why, all of a sudden, is this happening? He failed the test at the doctor's office. I was thinking, oh my God, could this be a tumor or something? Knowing I had little time before we were flying out of the country, I had to act fast. We took him to an emergency room and after failing three more eye tests, they decided to do a CAT scan on him. Yes, they actually did a CAT scan on my little guy. That's when I started to get really get worried.

Luckily they found nothing, but suggested he see an eye specialist. I got an appointment the day before we were leaving. I'm completely stressed. I still hadn't packed for three kids, I still needed to get all of the Christmas gifts wrapped, and we had a pick up time of 4 AM to go to the airport.

Tommy's appointment was at 3 o'clock. I figured he was going to need glasses and he would get a prescription. I figured we would be finished right around dinner time, so I had my husband meet me at the pizza place that was right across the street from the one hour eye glass place, with the twins. That way we could all eat while we waited for Tommy's new glasses. After major testing, eye drops, mirrors, letter and number guessing.

The doctor took Tommy out of the room, nicely asked the nurse to take him to the play area. He closed the door quietly, took one look at me, and said, "Your kid's faking it!" I didn't even bat an eye (no pun intended). I immediately knew he was right! My son had faked his blindness on four eye tests. How could he be so clever and pull the wool over my eyes? (Pun intended.) How could he have lied to me? Well, I know how he could have lied to ME...but to all those doctors and nurses! All for a little attention? The nerve of that child.

I was so furious at him! And I was mad at myself. Why didn't I see that coming! (Again, no pun intended.) I was so involved with Christmas, this cruise, and curing my kid that I panicked! I didn't do my own *Mean Mommy* rule, WAIT THREE DAYS! I was so stressed thinking about getting it all done that I didn't wait three days before I acted on anything. Instead, I put myself through hell, put him through a CAT scan, and I put my whole family in crisis mode. Needless to say, our family was a sight for sore eyes at the pizza place. (Sore eyes! Get it?)

Everyone in the joint could plainly see (even Tommy) that this family had some major issues to work out. So after all the tears, embarrassment, and lectures over pizza, we rushed home to get everything together for our trip. I had to pack and make sure the house was ready for when we got back – on Christmas Eve.

The alarm went off at 3:30 AM. We get everyone up and ready to go! It's a new day and we're going off on a cruise. I knew it was going to be a good day when Harry didn't throw up on the van ride down to the airport. I couldn't believe it. The guy was driving like a maniac, and I almost threw up. Tom was booked on an earlier flight because his travel was done by his manager. So, we dropped him off at his terminal. And to avoid paying for checked luggage, he gave me his suitcase because I could get one bag free per passenger. There were four of us, so I took Tom's luggage. We went to curbside checking and waited in line to get checked in. The guy looked at my son Cameron's passport and pointed to the expiration date. "You guys aren't going anywhere today, Ma'am," he said. His passport was expired!

All of a sudden, I'm getting pushed off to the side, with my four bags and three crying children. I immediately get on the phone with Tom. We were trying to discuss our options while our crying kids are in the background. There was no discussion, it was just yelling:

Tom: "I thought I told you to check the date on the passports!"

Kerri: "I did, but I only checked mine and we all got them at the same time, so I thought we were all fine!"

Tom: "Then what's the problem?"

Kerri: "The guy said that kids' passports expire every five years and adults' expire every ten."

Tom: "I've got to go to work, I can't cancel on them now, KERRI!"

Kerri: "I know, I know, I know THAT! I can't think, and the TSA guy is trying to move me out of the way and everyone's looking at me because I'm screaming at you and our kids are crying! It's freezing out here and one of our kids is banging his head on the street sign. Tommy! Tommy! Stop that! That really will make you go blind! STOP IT! TOMMY!!! Honey, what are we going to do?"

Tom: "Shit! YOU HAVE MY LUGGAGE! I need my suit for work. Get in a cab now and come to my terminal!"

Kerri: "I'm sorry, Tom! I'm sorry!"

Tom: "Don't be sorry! Just GET IN A CAB!"

I had mere minutes to get him his luggage so he could make his flight on time, and go on a cruise **without** his family.

I went into survival mode. I ignored my kids who thought they were going on a cruise and were now crying their little hearts out. I grabbed all our luggage and all our kids with my six arms and jumped in a yellow cab. "Terminal B – QUICK!" Then I got back on the phone to make sure Tom would meet me outside of the terminal because I was not about to get out with our kids AND our luggage to go find him. I dropped off the luggage just in time to kiss him good-bye and for him to make his flight.

Then I sat in that yellow cab with sobbing children in the back seat feeling defeated, discouraged, and demoralized. I tried to explain to them Life Happens, This Too Shall Pass, We Shall Overcome, and all that moral stuff, but I didn't even believe it myself. So, I just gave up. I was working on 3 hours sleep and I was crushed.

"Hey, Tommy at least now you can go to Pajama Day at school!" I said.

"What?! We're going to school? You're making us go to school, NOW?" More tears.

Once the sobbing subsided enough to think, the adding started in my head. The meter read $130.00 and we were only halfway home.

"Mom, I don't feel good…" I knew, from the sound of his voice, without turning around, who it was and what it was. It was Harry. And he was about to throw up.

"Cab driver, please pull over!?" I grabbed a shopping bag I found on the floor gave it to him just in time. Then the cab pulled over, Harry crawled out, finished what he had to do, and we continued our trip of shame back home. Then the adding started again in my head. *Now, I really have to tip this guy for the throw up in his cab. Should I make them go to school? We*

will be back in plenty of time for them to make the bus and I really
need that time to comprehend what had just happened. How much
money do I have in my wallet? How much do you tip on a cab ride
that cost 250.00? He was on the phone the whole time. I know he was
complaining about my kid throwing up in his car. It was in a different
language, but I could have sworn I heard "vomitar" a few times and
I'm pretty sure that means vomit in another language.

When we finally arrived home, I was so worried about paying the guy, getting my son's throw up bag out of the cab, and
all of our luggage, that I forgot the bag that had our camera
and video equipment in it, on the floor in the front seat of
the cab. I got the kids off to school, like the **Mean Mommy** that
I am and I called my "go to" friend, hoping she can get out
of work for a little while to meet me for coffee and walk me
through the hell that just happened.

So I'm not on the Promenade Deck with my fancy pina
colada, but I do have a medium hot latte waiting for me from
a supportive friend, and that's exactly what I needed. So, right
when I was telling her the part about the passports, I suddenly
realized that I had not only left thousands of dollars' worth of
equipment in the front seat of the cab, but that my whole life
was in there, too. Things that could never be replaced! "Did
you get the receipt?" she asked. I knew I liked her for a reason!
Thank God for BFF's. Luckily, in all of my scrambling around
trying to get outta that stupid cab, I did manage to take the
receipt with me, which had the phone number and the ID of
the cab driver. The ONE thing I did right! The ONLY thing
I did right! We got a hold of him, and before you know it, I'm
driving back into the city to meet with the cab driver to get my
precious stuff back. I couldn't have sat down for ten seconds
with my friend? I couldn't have taken a nap to catch up on the

hours of sleep I had lost the night before from packing for no reason? Instead of resting at a luxurious hotel on some remote island, I'm driving into the city hoping and praying I get my stuff back. Now the adding is beginning in my head again. *How much should I tip this guy for coming back into the city to meet with me and for not stealing my very expensive camera and computer equipment? Do I even have cash left in my purse?*

The story ends with my camera and video equipment safely back from New York City. The kids are safely back from school and Tommy's still in his PJ's and ready for bed.

The lesson: Don't let the holidays get you so stressed that you forget who you are. Be the *Mean Mommy* that you've always been and let your kid be blind for at least three days!

The silver lining: I now know that children's passports expire every five years. My kid is not blind, he doesn't have a tumor, he's just a great actor, and/or a lying little stinker!

The story: This one will go down in infamy with our family. It will be one of the stories that we will tell time and again and laugh our asses off.

MEAN MOMMY ON
DISNEY VACATIONS

When a woman comes back from vacation looking well rested, thinner, no wrinkles, with a glow about her, and a smile that just can't seem to go away, she just got back from plastic surgery.

When a woman comes back from a vacation looking exhausted, with blood shot eyes, a little puffy, and a smirk on her face, she just got back from Vegas.

When a woman comes back from a vacation looking tired, disheveled, bloated, disoriented and broke, she just got back from Disney World with her kids.

EAT YOUR EFFIN' BROCCOLI!

Do you realize that when you cook for the family it's never really what you want? What can I cook that's easy, the majority will eat, and I won't have an argument throughout dinner? Does that meal even exist? You try to make something yummy and healthy but you end up making a mistake. And how do you make your children eat broccoli? Why won't children eat their broccoli, but they'll pick their nose and eat it? I guess we should just put boogers on it and tell them to eat it.

No use trying to be fancy and bend over backwards for your kids. If you want your kids to eat something, go old school. Get back to the basics and just do what your parents did... "You don't have to eat your dinner, but if you don't you won't have dessert or anything else. So either you eat what's on your plate or not at all." Yes, it's mean! Your parents did it and you're fine so it can't be that mean. God forbid parents nowadays make their kids do something they don't like. Your kids aren't going to starve from not eating one night and believe me after that long night of the tummy growling they'll be eating what's on their plate the next day. I would always make them at least take one bite of it before I would throw it out. "There are poor kids in China that are starving for God's sake!"

If they get smart and say, "I already tried that and I know I don't like it so I'm not trying it again!" I go into an explanation of how your taste buds change and that you may have developed a new taste for it and I make them try it again. Sure enough the kid tries it and still hates it.

Or you think you know what they like, and you're all eating in harmony for a few weeks, they all of a sudden they stop liking it. "What happened? You used to love these!" Then the smarty-pants says to you, "Mom you said it yourself, 'your taste buds change!'" #StuckWithACaseOfElliosPizza

Dinner time is always so special in my house. I love it when our family gets together and we all sit at the table, say our prayers, and have great conversation about our wonderful day. The kids lend a helping hand setting the table and cleaning up after dinner. My husband and I have a nice relaxing glass of wine to wind down form a hard day's work. Then we go watch the news together by the fire while our wonderful kids start the dishwasher. #saidKerriNever

I usually find something quick that I can heat in the microwave then ask the boys to help set the table. That's when the yelling begins. It doesn't start off yelling, but the kids can never hear me the first time or they don't do it the first time or they do it half-assed and then they do a disappearing act. The dinner is ready, the table is half set and kids are nowhere to be found, not to mention that my husband isn't home when he said he was going to be. I told them all to get their drinks and they didn't. "Boys, where are you – it's dinner time! We have to eat fast because we're already running late for practice!" Finally, when the burnt food is all cold, we sit down for dinner. Now the whining begins:

"Do I have to eat that?"

"What is that?"

"My meat is cold."

"I don't like that sauce."

"My food is touching each other!"

And that's just my husband's complaining.

The kids are screaming, "Where's the drinks?" That's when I lose it!

"I told you all to get your own drinks and no one listened to me. SO NO DRINKS FOR YOU, NOW! JUST SHUT UP, EAT AND GET IN THE CAR!"

Can you imagine if I spent hours and really worked hard at cooking a perfect meal? I would have killed myself or at the very least tried to choke myself on the perfect meal I prepared.

Things go better when I pretend to be the cool mommy when I am really just the lazy mommy. "Okay kids tonight we're having breakfast for dinner! What kind of cereal do you want? Get a paper bowl!" or "Who wants to order Domino's?" or "Let's have some fun tonight, let's pretend that were stuck on an island with nothing to eat."

MEAN MOMMY ON ALLOWANCE

Mommy's little sweatshops: Start teaching them how to clean up before they can even talk. The sooner you get this done, the more time you have to go shopping for clothes that eventually your children will have to wash and fold for you. I don't think you should give your child allowance for the stuff they need to do around the house because they're part of the family. Yes, praise them give them rewards. But, don't give them money!

Let the neighbors pay them when they do a good job shoveling their walkway or babysitting their kids. I love it when my kids have a birthday party to go to or plans with their friends because my house is always clean. Mom can we go? Sure you can, but not until you room is clean and the play room is picked up. I've never seen little feet and hands move so fast. #Nowirehangers!

MEAN MOMMY ON BACK-TO-SCHOOL

When I was a kid, back-to-school shopping meant I was going to get some cool new jeans and sneakers. Depending on my mother's mood and finances that month, I might even get a pair of brand name sneakers. Oh, I prayed to the "Sneaker Gods" for that cool pair of Nike, Converse high tops, or Adidas to be on sale that day. Maybe I'd come home with a notebook or two, and the shopping was done. It was fun and I was back to the beach.

Back-to-school shopping has taken on a whole new meaning. Now that I have kids I hate back-to-school shopping. Fighting with them over why they're not getting the jeans that make them look like they're in a gang is the least of my worries.

I get a list of school supplies that I have to buy for my children and it's all due on the first day of school. Where was this list when I was a kid? We didn't have these lists. In school, we had an endless supply of markers, pencils (already sharped) and crayons. We had lots of scissors in a coffee can. None of them worked but they were free. Even the lefty kids had their own scissors.

Due to budget cuts, parents have to get all the supplies. They send out the list early so you have the whole summer to get them, but being the organized mother that I am, I waited until the day before school started. I thought it would be easy. I would just get all the supplies at the dollar store, but then I realized that I didn't want to be known as the "cheap mommy" on the very first day of school.

They needed three-ring binders, note books, pencil cases, highlighters, folders, plastic page protectors, tissues, Purell hand sanitizer and two packages of twenty #2 pencils. That led to some jokes from my two oldest. "Why are we writing while we're doing #2? Do we have to get these pencils in public Mom? I don't do #2 in school, I wait until I get home. These pencils smell like #2!"

I pretended I was annoyed with their sophomoric behavior, but deep down inside I thoroughly enjoyed it. I stopped laughing when I realized they had to be sharpened. Two packages of twenty, times two kids. Do that math…That's 80 pencils that need to be sharpened by the end of the night.

On my youngest son's list was a package of purple construction paper. I had to go to five different stores to get a package of purple construction paper. No stores had the color purple. They all had red – why couldn't my son get red construction paper on his list? *I swear I almost called Oprah to get the color purple.*

Finally I needed Clorox bleach wipes. Clorox? What? Are we cleaning for the schools now, too? Did the janitor's budget get cut, too? Next thing you know we'll all be donating gas cards for the principal to get to school. Six hours and $93.35 later, we got our supplies.

The money doesn't stop there. Don't even get me started on the fundraisers that will be coming in my children's book bag on a daily basis. Join the PTA! Our school needs money! Let's get a new playground! And I love this one, let's raise money for the school's yearbook. Yearbook? My kid is in first grade. He doesn't need a hardcover leather-bound year book so kids who can't even spell can write, "Dud! Hav a grate somer!"

Don't get me wrong, I love the first day of school! I've been waiting for this day for three months. I had all their first day of school outfits laid out, all their book bags are packed, and their lunches were made. I was ready, but we were up all night sharpening pencils so everyone overslept, and we missed the bus.

HUSBAND BASHING:
THE GUILTY PLEASURE

Women want guidance when it comes to bringing up our little, spoiled rotten, fart infested, snot factories – *but it's too late to help our husbands.*

People always ask me, "What's it like living with a husband who's a comedian? It must be so fun!" Yeah... no. I hate my husband just like every other normal married couple does. I'm kidding. I don't hate him. It's just when he breathes, that bothers me.

And why can't he put a dish in the sink? I'm not even asking him to wash it off and put it in the dishwasher. All I'm saying is that if you're finished with your dish, just put it IN the sink. Not right next to the sink, not hanging over the sink. In the GODDAM sink! How difficult is that? Apparently, it's very difficult for my husband. He would much rather put it 2 1/2 inches away from the sink and leave it there until the sink fairies come and push it into the sink.

My husband also has a hard time trying to think where an item might be before he yells out my name for five minutes.

Why won't he take a second to think about where it might be before he screams, "Hey honey? Sweetie! Muffin Cakes!!! Where are the batteries?"

Duh, in the battery drawer.

He says, "I didn't know we had one of those."

It says batteries right on it! It's been there for five years now. For five years you didn't know the batteries were in this drawer!? I know you think the batteries are in my bed side table...and you're right...but they're probably dead by now. Okay, occasionally I will put something away where it shouldn't be, but that's my little way of letting him know he can't live without me! #smileface

I'm married to the unfinished project man. He starts a project and never finishes it. I have little unfinished projects all over my house. He likes to assemble stuff in the living room so he can watch TV. Not in the garage where his work bench is. No he would rather watch TV than read the manual. I don't know why they call it a MAN-ual. I've never seen a MAN read one.

He never puts anything away and he never throws anything away! He calls me Patty Put Away and when he can't find something he starts to scream, "Hey Patty Put Away, where'd you put the stuff I left on the counter last week with my sandwich and a piece of cheese? It was right here last week where did it go? Patty? PATTY!" He gets so mad when I put his stuff away. If I don't it will sit there for years! I wish I had someone to follow me around and pick up my shit! I wouldn't get mad at them! I would smile and say thank you. And why won't he throw anything away? If you're not going to use it, THROW IT AWAY!

It took me 13 years of marriage to realize that my husband doesn't eat left-overs. He would always tell me to wrap it up for later. Then he would let it sit in the refrigerator for three weeks until I finally threw away the green, molded, fuzzy white thing that we can no longer recognize as food.

He does the same thing with his T-shirts. He has so many T-shirts that he can't even open his drawer. They're all faded with yellow arm-pit stains and they're gross. He never wears them, but God forbid I give them to Goodwill. He can't throw them away, just in case he might want to wear them one day.

That has my fraternity letters on it.

That was the year of the travel soccer playoffs.

We almost won the whole thing that year.

We came in 4th place, I'll never forget it!

I almost scored. I have to keep that one.

I love it when my husband wants to fix me when I'm upset. Does yours do that? It's so cute to watch. Men cannot fix women when we're upset. We can't even fix ourselves when we're upset and when we say nothing's wrong, it's because NOTHING IS WRONG! We're not lying to you!

If by any chance a guy is reading this you should know that whatever you do to try to fix us, it's wrong...but you have to try, I guess. You guys think it's easy to fix us. Like you can go to Home Depot, get a hammer and saw and fix us. Get a little duct tape and you're done! Duct tape will shut us up, but it won't fix us. You need to know that no matter what you do, it's wrong. If you talk to us, that's wrong. If you don't talk to us, that's wrong. If you touch us, well that's wrong. If you don't touch us, that's wrong. If you stay, that's wrong. If you go, that's wrong. You are WRONG! WRONG! WRONG! I tell my husband, go ahead leave me for someone prettier, smarter, and YOUNGER. It will be fun for the first few months maybe even a half a year, but then she's going to turn into a nagging, ugly face, crazy bitch just like me. We're all the same psycho, hormonal species so good luck with that! #takeyourlaundry

But my husband keeps asking me.

"What's wrong?"

"Nothing."

"Why are you so quiet?"

"Nothing's wrong."

"Well, you're slamming plates so something must be wrong"

Then I start thinking of things that happened ten years ago. "I'll tell you what's wrong. When we first dated you said you liked blondes. I'm not a blonde. Don't think that I'm changing my hair color for you, I'm not! And another thing – most people have plans. We don't have a plan, we don't know if we're coming or going. We should have a plan. All our neighbors do weekend projects we NEVER do weekend projects, and I FEEL FAT! THAT'S IT, I FEEL FAT, AND I'M STARVING!"

Every woman knows what if feels like to be fat. Guys never know what it feels like to feel fat, even the fat guys never know what is feels like to feel fat. But women, no matter what size we are, we have three sizes of jeans in our closets. Our skinny jeans, our normal jeans and our period fat jeans. If we are in our period fat jeans and it's not our period, IT'S A BAD DAY! (Period) I want to be buried in my skinny jeans when I die. Tell my husband in case he never reads this chapter. I want to be buried in my skinny jeans when I'm dead and I finally lose all that water weight! He knows where they are – bottom of the pile of jeans. I want to look hot when I'm dead so bury me in those and just those. I may need a bustier or something, because when I don't have my bra on my boobs are down to my knees and I'm not even dead yet. Can you imagine what they would look like when I'm lying in the coffin? So I would need like a really nice bedazzled, underwire bustier to hold it all up there and my skinny jeans. That's the way to die.

What kills me is that Bruce Jenner worked so hard to become Caitlin! I give her a few years then she's going to be like, "This sucks! My feet are killing me. I have to do my hair every day, my skin is bad from wearing this make-up, and this wrinkle cream doesn't work. Everyone's jealous of me because I'm prettier than they are!" Now the former Olympic gold medalist can't even keep up with the Kardashians.

I haven't even started talking about when you leave your husband home with the kids! First of all, when you've left them with your husband for only two seconds, that means you have to spend at least four hours re-teaching and retraining your kids not to do what Daddy just did.

Second of all, don't expect anything to get done while you're gone. They are not multi-taskers like us. They can only take care of the kids. They can't clean up, vacuum, switch over the wash, feed the fish, tell the kids to clean up one game before moving to the next, or pick up the dry-cleaning on the way to soccer practice. They can only do one thing. So, if you leave your kids home with your husband to get a few things done, go shopping, or better yet, get a spa treatment – make sure you know that when you get home you'll have a lot more to do and get done. So ask yourself, is this worth it? The answer is always, NO! But, go anyway!

If you mention that maybe he can go get the kids haircuts while you're away, it will go like this...

Wife: So maybe while you're out you can swing by the barber shop and get the kids haircuts?

Husband: What? You're adding things at the last minute and that was not in the plan.

Wife: It's not last minute and we're making the plan now.

Husband: Well, I've got a million things to do while you're gone!

Wife: What do you mean? All you have to do is take Tommy to his basketball game at 3 and it ends at 4.

Husband: Well, I don't know if I can fit it in, I'll try.

Wife: Forget it! Just keep them alive until I get home.

Lastly, and this is what pisses me off the most, the kids like him best! He's the fun guy! He's the YES MAN! They would rather stay with him than me. My kids have a blast with him. I'm always the *Mean Mommy*! I know I wrote a book titled *Mean Mommy* but that doesn't mean I really want to be *The Mean Mommy*! Why can't I be the fun mom, too? Because I'm always the one working hard planning everything so we can have fun daddy time.

I've come to the conclusion that I will wait until my children grow up and come to the epiphany that I am actually the fun one. That in actuality it was me that did all the work to make it all happen. That is was ME that actually kept them safe, healthy and alive so they could have fun. As an adult and especially after I had my own kids, I came to the conclusion that, all those fun times and all those special moments I had with my father would have never been possible if it wasn't for my mother. (I love you Mom. Now I'm crying! See I'm never any fun!)

Speaking of YES MAN, my husband says yes to anything and anyone who asks him to do something. His friends call him up to go golfing – Yes! Another comic calls him up to go to the movies – YES! His manager asks him to go to Hong Kong for three weeks of fun and one night of work – YES! Without missing a beat he gets to say YES! I, on the contrary, have to go through a spreadsheet in my head before I can say

YES! What are my kids doing during that time? Where's my husband going to be? Can I get babysitter with a car? And do I trust her to drive my kids? Can I get a parent to give them a ride? Will it be meal time when I go? Will I miss any doctor appointments or school plays? And last but not least, is it worth saying YES? Is it worth being tired the next day, paying for a babysitter, having the dishes pile up, bothering my kids' friends' mothers for rides and sleepovers?

Wouldn't it be wonderful if you could just say YES without thinking about anything else but yourself! Wouldn't it be wonderful if you could all of a sudden just say to everyone in your family, Bye, I'm leaving, fend for yourselves! I dream about doing that someday! I really do, but then I know that no one would survive without me, so I don't. I escape by writing this chapter bashing my husband instead. We don't have to go to couples therapy, and I feel better. Oh by the way, one more thing...if I ask him to go to couples therapy, that's when the YES MAN becomes the NO MAN!

Okay, one more thing and I swear I'll stop. He manscapes way longer than I do! Forty-five minutes in the mirror and he still looks the same! #NoNoseHairForTheYesMan

If you want your marriage to last forever – never expect anything from your husband. Ever. If you expect it, it won't happen. If he does do it, it won't be done the way you want it to be done and you'll have to do it over again.

If you don't expect it and he does it you're like, "Oh my... who is this big, beautiful, man in my house? I think I will have sex with him tonight." That's a good feeling to have. So, lower your expectations.

MEAN MOMMY ON WHY I HATE BIRTHDAY PARTIES

The Big Expensive Birthday Party: Laser tag, bowling, trampoline parties, bouncy houses. They cost at least 15 bucks a kid and that's without the necessary extras: the party room, video games, bonus play time and (God forbid) the child molester in the rat suit singing to the children.

The 1st Birthday Party: Why do parents spend all this money, time, and effort for their baby's first birthday party? The baby will never remember it. Which is just as well since Uncle John will undoubtedly get drunk again. #WhoInvitedUncleJohn

The Three Extra Siblings tagging along to the party that you didn't account for, and now you have to pay for, because their mother felt bad leaving them home.

If You Don't Invite The Whole Class You Can't Send Invitation in to School. So the school policy makes you spend hours finding names and addresses, to not hurt anyone's feelings. Only you find out that these little snots can't keep their mouths shut and they end up talking about the party anyway.

<u>Buying Extra Food For The Parents</u>. If you don't have food for the parents they will complain. If you have food for them, none of them eat it. #Cruditesfor20

<u>Late Picker Uppers</u>: It's always the same pain-in-the-ass kid whose parents can't stay and then are late picking him up. That's the same kid who has the food allergies and can't eat the cake. And here's a shocker...that's the same parents who never RSVP'd.

<u>The Snot-Nosed Birthday Boy</u> who tries to blow out the magic prank candles that never go out. He's getting his saliva all over the cake until finally someone yells out, "LET'S EAT!" #soggycake

<u>All The Gifts Your Kid Receives</u> are the gifts that you wouldn't have let him have in the first place.

<u>Having a House Party</u>. You might think you'll save money by having a few rug rats over to your house and cooking and cleaning and making everything yourself. Only to deal with the tsunami aftermath. I swear 7-year-olds can cause more damage to your house in an hour than a frat house can in a week.

<u>GOODIE BAGS</u>! We all hate getting them and they're filled with crap from the dollar store. The little pieces of the yo-yo will fall through the cracks of your car seat along with the melted off-brand chocolate they didn't eat. So let's stop the madness. Let's at least do one thing and pledge together as moms – NO MORE Goodie Bags!!

A LETTER TO MY FAMILY ON MOTHER'S DAY

Dear loving, messy children and wonderful, trying husband,

All I want for Mother's Day this year is for you ALL to get the hell out of the house and leave me alone. Yes, all of you. Including the dog. Okay, I know we don't have a dog, but if we did he's out, too.

I love you all very much. Words can't describe my undying, unconditional and total love for all of you but, for this Mother's Day, I want to be left alone for at least 9 hours...maybe even 10.

To my dearest husband, on this special day I don't want a gift of any kind. I don't need or want anything except for me to be in our house alone! I don't want to hear, "Honey," "Sweetie," and I don't want to hear:

"Where's the car keys?"

"Do WE have sugar in the house?"

"Did WE do laundry?"

"Do WE have our trip planned out yet?"

When what you're really trying to say is:

"Why are YOU hiding the car keys?"

"What were YOU doing all day that YOU couldn't get sugar at the store?"

"Did YOU do the laundry?"

"Did YOU plan and pack for our vacation yet?"

To my adoring children, I especially don't want to hear any of these words on Mother's Day this year:

> mommy
> mom
> mother
> maaaha
> I want
> you're mean
> that's not fair
> please mom
> pretty please
> he did it
> how come
> it wasn't me
> or
> I hate you!

I don't want to hear any whining, crying or begging. That's why we don't have a dog. I hate begging.

Mother's Day is a celebration of the very fact that I am the mother of you three beautiful children. I'm with you every second of every day so every day is like Mother's Day to me. Every day is special. Why not change it up a bit and leave mommy alone for just one day so she can reflect on how much she loves you.

Don't get me wrong, I will miss the breakfast in bed. I will be thinking about the cardboard toast, rubber eggs, and pancakes drenched in syrup. I will miss the hours it takes me to put my kitchen back together again after you three, awesome cooks took it over for one morning. I will miss doing laundry because no matter how careful you are someone always gets syrup all over the sheets. I will miss cleaning up when the oversized cup you found to put the orange juice in spills all over my bedside table.

So this Mother's Day you don't have to do any of that stuff. You don't have to do anything, but get out of the house. Have fun!

LOVE, MOM

P.S. And please, for the love of God, don't come home with a dog.

MEAN MOMMY ON GETTING OUT OF THE HOUSE

Remember those days before you had kids? Getting out of your house was so easy. All you had to remember was your keys, money and ID. You didn't even have to remember your phone because there were no phones back then. (I'm talking to my older readers here, so you young folks shake that smirk off your face!) It's so hard to get out of your house no matter what the ages of your children are. It never gets easier, it just gets different!

When they're babies, the list goes on... you have to remember to pack your shit and all their gear. I would list it all, but that would take too much time and I would never finish writing this book let alone get out of my house.

When they're toddlers getting just their shoes on will take half an hour. When they're a little older and they can actually put their shoes on, it's still no help. Basically you're expecting them to go upstairs and put on their shoes. You did not calculate extra time for them to get distracted with the pile of dinosaurs on the floor that they forgot put away and come downstairs with no shoes on. Now you're late and everyone is going to think that you're the disorganized mommy.

When they're school age and if you have more than one kid, the shoes are on, but you hear the fighting: No, I want to wear the blue jacket! No I want to wear the blue jacket! No, I do, I had if first! So you try to referee, "Someone has to wear the red jacket so we can go. Come on let's go, the red jacket makes you look thinner, now, who wants to wear it? I have an idea let's flip a coin!"

Now more time is spent to look for a quarter then you hear, I'm heads! No, I'm heads! No, I am! I called it first! MA! So you referee again and because you're the master manipulator of all things it goes like this, "Pick a number from one to ten! You got it, you're wearing the blue one. LET'S GO!" Let's not, because now it's three o'clock in the afternoon and we missed it.

Sometimes I scream, "I'm getting in the car and I am leaving. If you're not in it, I'm leaving without you!" My *Mean Mommy* tactic seems to be working. I haven't figured out what I'm going to do when it doesn't work and I actually have to leave without them. Maybe drive around the cul-da-sac! I wish I could actually leave, but the cops say it's wrong.

When they're in high school or even worse, back home living with you after college, you can never get them out of your house. They'll be sleeping until one in the afternoon. Sure you get mad at them. Then you get melancholy because just a short time ago when they were newborns, you were praying for these little buggers to sleep in. Now you're yelling at them to get up and get out of the house!

CUTTING THE PINEAPPLE

I don't want to have sex. I want to look like I'm having sex. That's a Yummy Mommy. I want to be a Yummy Mommy. My husband would rather I was a MILF. He was on the computer, and I must tell you that he knows nothing about the computer. He always thinks the computer is broken and we have to get a new one when the volume doesn't work. *I'm like un-click mute, you moron, we're not buying a new computer.* So he shows me the site called MILF. He tells me that these cyber sluts are mothers. He explains that "Tina" has five kids and likes to play tennis in her free time. I tell him that these women couldn't possible be mothers. "They're way too young, way too skinny and not one of them has a stretch mark. And some of them have boobs that are bigger than an actual baby. They're not mothers!" Not to mention, no mother of 5 kids, ever in the history of motherhood, has ever had free time to play tennis. And if by chance she does have free time she's not playing tennis. If a mother finds herself with free time, she's sleeping. That's right she's in her bed under all the covers, bedroom door is locked, earplugs are in her ears, she's sleeping like a baby.

"Come on!" he says, "They're totally mothers, this one here has an identical twin who's a mom, too. Look, honey, look at the way they're posing together. How come you never get together with your sister like that?" I just sat there in awe and said, "You can't cut-n-paste, but you can download this crap?"

SEX! It's free, it's fun, you lose weight while doing it, and it only takes a minute. (Well, only a minute if you're with my husband.) So why is it that we don't do it more often? Why is it that every time I finally get around to having sex with my husband, we both say at the same time, "Wow why don't we do that more often?" Why don't we? Why does it feel like it's just another thing I have to do? Having sex is like going to the gym. You have so much to do and it's the last thing you want to be doing, you don't think you have enough time to fit in a full session, and you can always just do it tomorrow. But when you put that outfit on and actually do IT, you feel so much better about yourself and you're so glad you did it. I don't know why I just don't drop everything I'm doing, go to the man of my dreams, the Emperor of my world, and f–k his brains out? (*Well, because I'm married and Ryan Gosling lives in L.A.*) Why can't I just switch gears from motherhood to wife and go have sex in a second's notice? Before kids, I could. But there is so much more to do on the TO DO LIST and so little time. (My husband is not on the To Do List.) This is what goes on in my mind: *I could just go to bed now and have sex with my husband or... I could do the laundry and if I do it now, it won't be backed up tomorrow. The dishwasher has to be emptied and filled and then emptied and filled again. I have got to take a shower. Tomorrow is my early day. Do I have a sinus infection? Plus I have to vacuum the whole house, because I already put it off for three days. Boy, that ceiling fan is dusty. Are my armpits shaved?*

As mothers we are constantly doing things for others and constantly thinking of others. We must make a conscious effort to change this and the way we think. We can start by communicating with our husbands. Tell them what we're feeling, even the absurd: He may not know that emptying the dishwasher equals sex. I'm sure if guys knew that the simple, yet daunting task of emptying the dishwasher will equal sex, then all the dishwashers around the world would be empty. But you must put in fine print that this is not always the case, and could be subject to change, at any given time, without notice.

The less I have sex, the less I want it or even think about it. It's out of sight out of mind for me. For guys it's different. The less they have sex the more they want it. That being said, if you want more sex in your relationship you need to practice, practice, practice. Guys do all the time. If you want to have more quality sex and you want to have more orgasms, then as with everything, you have to get good at it by practicing. The best way you can practice and get good at it is by doing it yourself. Yes, just like everything, if you want it done right, you have to do it yourself!

Masturbation – that's what I'm talking about. I hate that word... masturbation... it sounds so sick and naughty. I always think of some old guy in a trench coat in a dark alley jerking off. That's disgusting! Which is why I hate saying that word masturbation. There, I just said it again. From now on can't we just say cutting the pineapple? I have no idea what that means, but it sounds better.

My husband works out of town a lot, so there are plenty of times when I should be playing with myself, or as some male comics I know might put it, "greasing the tracks for when he returns." My husband actually bought me a vibrator for when he's away. Which, I recommend for all women. However, I don't use mine as much as I should and I forget most of the time, but when I do use it I'm glad I did. But I have no idea where it is – probably collecting dust in one of my sock drawers. I should find it before one of my kids accidentally finds it. I can see it now, "Mommy, you didn't tell us you have a light saber! It looks different – is it Darth Vader's? It's not working, Mommy, can you put batteries in this? I think it needs a double D!" #That'sWhatHeSaid.

I want to have a sex toy party. Those are fun. I went to one a long time ago and never bought anything and now that I'm older and my "don't give a crap factor" is higher, I think I just might buy a few things this time. If you haven't gone to one, you must go to one or do one yourself. And if you can't do one yourself, make your best friend do it. My whole neighborhood has been asking me to have one because they're all teachers and bookkeepers and God forbid they have a sex party. "You're the comedian – you have it!" they say. I would much rather have one of these parties then a Pampered Chef party. Make sure you know what party you're going to. You don't want to get a sex party and a Pampered Chef party mixed up. Some of the useful things do look alike. So when the lady is holding up a turkey baster you don't accidentally say, "So how many speeds does that have on it?" The best part about hosting a party is that the more your friends buy, the more stuff you get free, so be sure to invite all your slutty friends.

Note to self: find more slutty friends. #Classof87

So I was lying in my bed alone one random night thinking I need to sleep right now because I have an early morning, but

I'm too stressed to just fall right to sleep. I'm too busy thinking of all the things I need to do. I could take Tylenol PM, but I'm too lazy to get out of bed and that takes a few more minutes to get into my bloodstream. Hmm, maybe I should just play with myself... that always puts me to sleep. It's safer than an Ativan drip, it's cheaper, and I'm less likely to get addicted. I tried to get the job done and nothing happened. So much for me getting to sleep, and if I didn't have anxiety two minutes ago, I do now. I can't even get the job done by myself. It's one thing if I'm with my husband it's another thing when I'm by myself. *Oh God, is there something wrong with me? I'm about to have one of those really big numbered birthdays - you know the ones. The ones that people get you stupid funny old geezer gifts for, instead of what you really need, anti-wrinkle cream. So I thought, Oh My God, am I too old? Is something wrong with me? I'm drying up! Should I get up and get the KY Jelly? Well if I do that I might as well just take the Tylenol PM because it's right next to the KY Jelly. I'm not getting out of bed. I'm too tired. Oh God does that mean I'm depressed, too? Am I going through early menopause? Will I ever have sex again? Will I ever be in the mood ever again?*

I told my husband and he said, "Don't worry, you're fine. I'll empty the dishwasher when I get home."

The next afternoon, I was driving to a comedy gig. The show was about five hours away. To you that might be a long drive. Well, not when you've been with kids 24/7. I was looking forward to the drive. I hadn't had a gig this far away in a long time and it would be good to just get away from it all and be alone in the car for that long. The first hour was just decompressing. I purposely shut the radio off and was loving the quietness of just me and the open road. The next hour I actually could hear myself think and I had some pretty good thoughts. The third hour I put the music up full blast and I danced my ass off. I was singing at the top of my lungs and I thought I sounded good for a minute. I was dancing and singing like a wild "American Idol" 21-year-old. Really you should ask the truckers who beeped at me and thought I was some kind of lunatic. No, just a mom without her kids for the first time in a long time.

I was very much relaxed, no one asking me questions, and no mouths to feed. My mind was clear. The only discomfort I had was that I had to go to the bathroom. I don't know what it was, but with my bladder being full and all those bumps on the road I was feeling something going on down there. (Down there = vagina) "Wow," I thought, "it feels good – I haven't felt this in a long time. I have to take advantage of this moment especially since I couldn't get the job done the other night. I have to prove to myself that I'm not old and drying up. I have to do something about this feeling. But I can't, I'm driving in my car."

People have done it in their cars before. It's not that uncommon. But how can I do it in the car when I couldn't even do it in my own bed. Just give it a try, I thought to myself. So I made sure not to pass any of those truckers and – let's just say I cut some pineapple and I got the job done! I did it! Wow, it felt good. I was proud of myself for not stomping on this feeling and taking care of myself. I was happy to finally make myself feel good, but felt weird at the same time. I can't believe I just cut the pineapple in a car while driving!! I felt alive. I felt naughty and silly. I had to tell someone. But who? I immediately called my best friend in the whole entire world and said, "TOM, HONEY, GUESS WHAT? I'M BACK IN ACTION!!" He said, "Thank God, because I forgot to empty the dishwasher."

True story. Unless of course you're my mother, then I made it up, but if you're my mother and you're reading this then you got a hold of someone else's book, because I took this chapter out before I gave you your signed copy of this book.

The point I'm trying to make is (I know you're thinking, "Oh thank God there's a point to all this –") if your life is so hectic you hardly have sex and you want to have more of it then you have to first find out what it is that motivates you to want to have sex, communicate that to your spouse, and both of you make it your priority. When you're a mother, sex is the last thing on your mind, but if you want more of it and your husband wants more of it, then put it on the TO DO LIST. If it takes both of you getting your calendars out to plan it, then do that. If you always fall asleep right after the movie you watch together then plan on having sex before the movie. Do it in the morning if that's going to work for both of you. It doesn't always have to be at night after dinner and a movie. Think of the benefits – if you do it before dinner you can eat whatever you want and who cares if you feel bloated – you already had sex!

I'm sorry to say, it has nothing to do with my husband, how he looks or what he does to turn me on, if I don't feel sexy and I have a lot on my mind then it's a waste of time. Whatever it is that's going to make you feel fabulous then make it your priority. No one is going to make you feel good about yourself but you. Every mother should be able to feel fabulous and sexy. Every mother should be made to feel like she's irresistible.

But why not just let your husband think that it was all him. You don't want him thinking that you had anything to do with your own orgasm. Let him think that he was just too tempting and that you couldn't help yourself. Yes, let him think that he was the sexiest thing you've ever seen. The way he smelled, the way he touched you, and looked at you. But most importantly, let him think that it was the size of his penis that magically turned you into a Yummy Mommy that night.

MEAN MOMMY ON GETTING
YOUR KID INVOLVED

I 'm a firm believer in getting your children involved in activities. When children get into trouble it's mostly because they're bored. So it's a must to get them involved in something. But it's getting out of control, especially with sports, and I blame the parents. Do we really need to hear that a parent beat up a coach in front of everybody on the football field because their 7-year-old kid didn't get enough playing time. Really?

Whenever I get my kid involved in a sport or an extracurricular activity and I see that the parents and the coaches are too intense, I pull them out. Some parents believe that if your kid doesn't come out of the womb kicking a soccer ball then forget it, it's too late.

Instead of having it drilled in their heads that they love it, let them discover it. I'm all for getting your kid involved and, if they love something and want to live and breathe it, by all means get them involved, but make sure they're not getting stressed out and missing out on life. You're probably thinking that I'm just saying this because my kids suck at sports. That may be true – but that's not the point.

DON'T EVER ASK A WOMAN IF SHE'S PREGNANT, EVER!

When I had my twins I didn't have a really big belly until the last two months of pregnancy, When I had my second baby, my belly got big right away and then kept getting bigger. I was bigger with my one baby than I was with two babies. My belly knew exactly what is was like being pregnant so I popped out fast and then kept going. I was so big my belly button was flat which was good because that's the first time it's ever been clean.

After all these years my belly just remembers what it's like to be stretched out and pregnant so I still look pregnant! I don't look fat, I look pregnant. The skinner I get the more pregnant I look. If I'm getting my period and if I haven't pooped in a while, I swear to God I look four months pregnant. Even I thought I was pregnant one night looking and feeling my baby pouch. I made my husband go and get me a pregnancy test. It was negative, but I'm still worried because he got it at the dollar store. I've been working my ass off trying to get my ass off!

Throughout my pregnancy with my twins I was Super Woman. I was eating right, no caffeine, and I was teaching aerobics 4 to 5 times a week right up until I gave birth. Some of the club members were so nervous for me. "When are you going to stop working?" "Is this safe?" "Maybe you should take it easy?!" And I'm like, "I'm working out for three and I'm running circles around you so, I'd be more worried about me having to give you CPR when you collapse in the middle of my class." See, I told you I was Super Woman! After giving birth to my twins I worked really hard to lose my baby weight. It wasn't that hard since I didn't gain that much weight with the twins, however I basically had an 11 pound baby in there so needless to say my stomach stretched out. Then I did it again to myself four years later. Well, I didn't do it myself my husband had something to do with it. I gained more weight with my single baby than I did with my twins. This last child syndrome is killing me! My belly was so big, (how big was it?) It was so big, I had a belly ring and that flew off and hit my doctor in the eye. *I couldn't even bend over, which was how I got in the mess in the first place,* but we'll save that story for my next book *70 Shades Of Charcoal Gray, With a Touch of Silver.* So you get the picture. I was stretched out! No matter how hard I worked out, no matter how hard I concentrated on eating really healthy and clean, I would still look pregnant during that time of the month.

I didn't look fat I looked pregnant. The skinnier I got the more I looked pregnant! At some points I was so depressed and frustrated, I asked myself why am I trying so hard to look good, because when I do, I look pregnant. Why don't I just let myself go and put a little more weight on me, because that way my weight is evened out and I don't look as pregnant! But then I felt fat and I hated myself. I didn't fit into my clothes and believe me, I'm not about to get a whole new wardrobe especially if it's a size bigger!!! So I will just look pregnant! OH! That's a great alternative! I'm left with a choice of being three sizes bigger or looking pregnant? Hmmm, what to do? What to do? I was always constipated, so I always looked pregnant. I felt fat, I looked fat, I felt bloated, I was bloated. Depressed, unhappy, gloomy, and, sluggish. To add insult to injury, on the days when I was feeling all those things I got asked if I was pregnant. It sucked!

I really hated how I felt. I hated spending countless hours trying to find the right shirt that wouldn't make me look pregnant, be able to make me look thin, but hide my protruding belly. Then taking another twenty-five minutes to squeeze into those awesome Spanx I bought. I have a lump from my C-section, from all the scar tissue buildup. After all these years it's still numb and sensitive in that area. So finding pants that are comfortable can be daunting.

Sometimes you can see the C-section lump in my aerobic pants, while I'm teaching aerobics, in front of the wall-to-wall, ceiling-to-floor mirror. Why do I seek out jobs where I work in front of a mirror, in front of an audience, being judged constantly, and on a stage? Why can't I just be a normal person and hide quietly behind a desk, a computer, or a counter. I'm always uncomfortable, I'm always self-conscious, and no matter what I try to do, I'm never happy with the results. I hated that I was always bloated and constipated. I tried every laxative, probiotics, and the yogurt with probiotics. You know the one? The Activia that Jamie Lee Curtis sells in the park on that commercial. I never got that commercial. Why would she sell a probiotic in a park where there are no bathrooms in sight!

I've seen a proctologist who told me that my constipation, bloating, and protruding belly problem is normal. Anyway, I tried everything and I would still be bloated and gassy, I had gas in my shoulder blade. Yes, that's some really bad gas. Have you ever had gas in your shoulder blade? It hurts and there's no way out. I always knew I was full of shit, I just didn't realize I was literally full of shit! No doctors will tell you that a tummy tuck is a cure for constipation and it's probably not a cure, but I just knew that if they tightened my abdominal muscles then it would at least help things flow through a little smoother and help my sluggish intestines. That's what I was told I have lazy, sluggish bowels! So that's another major reason for me wanting a tummy tuck. You can't tell Super Woman she has lazy and sluggish bowels!

I get asked if I'm pregnant all the time. It's happened so many times, I sort of expect it now. I don't get asked by men – they're smart. They don't ask unless the woman admits she's pregnant. It's the women and the old people who just can't keep their mouths shut. They don't have filters. Older ladies were always asking me if I should be running around so much since I'm expecting. You try to tell them you're not pregnant and they can't hear you.

One old lady said to me, "Oh dear, is that a baby in there? You should take it easy; you didn't tell us you're having a baby!" They're so damn cute you can't get mad at them, but deep down inside you want to take their walkers and beat them over the head with it. The young women just get too excited and they lose all control. I've actually had one woman scream so loud everyone stopped what they were doing and looked over at me, "Oh My God ARE YOU pregnant!?" as she reached out to touch my belly! I was shaking my head No, then she saw the look on my face and it was too late. Her hand was already on my belly and we both just wanted to die. Needless to say everyone in the room wanted to die with us. One woman thought I was hiding the fact I was pregnant and started auguring with me. "Yes you are, just tell me, you're having a baby!" She thought she figured out my plan before anyone else and she was going to break the big secret. "Just tell me you're having your 4th child, aren't you?!" she said. "Is it a girl this time? It must be – you're carrying low."

Can you believe I had to argue with this woman about whether or not I was pregnant? I was trying to be polite, but inside I was saying to myself, "What part of NO I'M NOT PREGNANT don't you understand? I'm just fat, now take your foot and put it in your mouth before I gag you with it." Finally, she says she's sorry and that it must have been the shirt I was wearing or the way I was standing. (Believe me I've never worn that shirt again.) So to avoid humiliation, I just tell people I'm pregnant. It's a better conversation and no one feels like they want to die! "Wow!" this one woman said to me as I shook my head yes that I was indeed pregnant, "Kerri, you look great for 4 months." I said, "I know!" with a big smile on my face. You don't even look pregnant from behind," she says. I said, "I know!" with an even bigger smile on my face. I walk away happy she walks away jealous of me because I look so good pregnant and no one gets hurt. Unfortunately, she happened to be a lactation consultant. So now I have an interview with her the Tuesday after my fake baby's born, so she can help me breast feed.

So let me give you women and old people some advice, never ask a woman if she is pregnant. I don't care if she's looking like she just ate a basketball and she's rubbing her back. Don't ask her. I don't care if she has a foot hanging out of her hoo-hoo! Don't ask her, until she says, "You moron, I'm having a baby, call 911!" Then congratulate her, but call 911 first – that baby is breached, she's going to need some help.

If you're like me and you have a belly then here's my advice to you. Spend big bucks on a great pair of Spanx. I have the best Spanx. I'm talking the really expensive Spanx. Not the heavy duty, stretchy material kind. I'm talking the rubber tire, metal clips, it's not going anywhere, type of Spanx. It's like the corset of the millennium. So I bought mine and I love it. I look great. I can't breathe in it, but I look great. My clothes fit smooth and nothings poking out. If I really want to make sure I look good then on top of the Spanx I throw on my girdle that helps to hide those metal clips, and on top of that, some duct tape. I look fan-tab-ulous, just don't take me to bed because then it's going to be like, trying to open up one of those Pillsbury crescent roll cans. All of a sudden you hear POOF! And then it all comes flopping out! I hate those cans. You know that sound is coming and you think you're ready for it, but it scares the hell out of you every time. Those cans should come with a warning label. #DoughBoyAbs

MEAN MOMMY ON TALKING
TO STRANGERS

Your privates are private. No one can touch them, but you. No one! Unless Mommy needs to wash them, or auntie, or your Cousin Julia who babysits you. Oh yeah, Daddy too, but no one else. Oh yeah, your doctor can too, but only if Mommy is in the room. Tell your child not to talk to strangers, unless they have a really good knock off designer bag they're selling that would go great with Mommy's new shoes.

You can talk 'til you're blue in the face: "Don't talk to anyone trying to give you a candy or anyone who asks you to help them with their dog." You can practice and role play and every time they will do the right thing and not get in the car or go with you. Every time they will say the right answer – NO. Here's what I suggest: Tell your kids to trust their instincts. When they're too young to even know what that means tell them if something doesn't feel right or you feel something weird in your tummy, it's not right. Go get help. Go find your mommy.

As they got older I gave the same speech. I added in anything I could think of that might ever happen on the internet or social media pages, but even then you don't know what's out there. Especially the internet. You can't think of every possible scenario to protect your kid. So I always say this to my children, "Please listen to your heart, listen to your body, and trust your instincts if something doesn't feel right, something seems a little off, then it is! Stop what you're doing immediately and go get help."

One day I was playing on the floor with my little guy, Tommy who was two at the time, I said, "Tommy, remember no one is to ever touch you down there, you know that, right?" He said, "Yes, Mommy, I know, but if they do I'm going to tell them to keep doing it because it feels good!" I just shook my head knowing I have a lot of work to do with this one. Then I smiled and thought, *he's just like his father!* #TrustYourInstincts

HOWARD STERN GAVE ME A
TUMMY TUCK!

Not really. I mean he wasn't there with his scrubs ready to cut me open. He didn't have his surgical gloves on, wearing that little blue hat over his big curly head of hair. But because of Howard Stern, I had a tummy tuck.

What Howard actually did was become a fan of my comedian husband Tom Cotter, when he auditioned to be on the seventh season of *America's Got Talent*. Because of all the wonderful things Howard said throughout the competition, Tom went all the way to the finals. It was so exciting – it came down to him and a dog act! And of course he was going to win over a dog act, right?!

No, apparently America loves dogs. I have to admit they were really cute. One of the dogs did about 8 back flips in a row. They were so adorable, even I almost voted for them. My husband came in second place. He didn't win the competition or the million dollars, but it did change our lives forever.

Finally, my husband got the recognition he deserved for doing so well on that reality show and, because he almost won, he got lots of great gigs. I can't tell you how proud I am of him. After all the years of hard work, he was finally getting the respect he deserved. He was such a gentleman throughout the competition and not only was he funny as hell, he was humble! America fell in love with his loyalty, his vulnerability. They saw a loving father, and just an incredible human being. America saw the exact same guy I saw 25 years ago, and I married him. I got to witness my three boys watch America fall in love with their very own father. I got to witness firsthand the dreams that we've shared for a very long time finally come true.

Okay, enough mushy crap. I'll get on with the topic at hand, me and my tummy tuck! Or as I like to call it "Operation Mommy Fix Up." Because of the opportunities my husband got and because I was sick of always feeling bloated and people always asking me if I was pregnant, we decided to finally get me a tummy tuck.

At first, my husband thought I was crazy. Every time I would whine to him about feeling fat, wanting a tummy tuck, or some woman said I looked pregnant today, he would just say you're making this up, you don't look pregnant. You look great! He felt I was making a mountain out of a mole hill. He would just walk away and dismiss it. Until the day it happened right in front of him. Some woman asked us when "WE" were expecting. I ran away and left him to tell that poor woman that WE weren't pregnant. It wasn't until that moment that he could really feel my pain.

He thinks I look great the way I am, and loves me no matter what I look like. He wants me to be happy and he would support me if I got a tummy tuck. He really wants me to feel better about myself. He would always say, "Happy wife, happy life!"

My abdominal muscles separated because of my pregnancy with the twins and they'd never be back to where they were unless I had surgery to pull them back together again. My muscles being separated is a major cause to why I'm always bloated and constipated, too. You may look at me and say I look great and I shouldn't be complaining. You're right, I'm at a size some women would dream about. You may think there're so many women out there, far worse than I am, and you're right about that, too. But why shouldn't I feel better about myself? Why shouldn't my looks match the hard work and long hours I put in at the gym? Why shouldn't I feel healthier and more regular? I have spent hours working hard to avoid looking pregnant. I have been in the fitness industry for over two decades and I've taught aerobics until I was eight and a half months into both my pregnancies. I make sure I drink my water, take my vitamin, and stay healthy for my family and myself. I haven't had carbs in over two decades. (Okay that's a lie, wine has carbs in it.) You get the picture.

When my kids ask me why I'm cranky, it's hard to explain to them that mommy feels sad because someone had asked her if she was going to have a baby. I can't tell them that mommy feels fat, bloated, and she can't breathe because her corset is too tight. "Boys, Mommy is mean because she has to poop!" My kids deserve a mother who feels good about herself. My husband deserves a wife that's happy. I deserve to look like the fitness professional that I am and I should feel good when I'm performing on stage. It's hard to make people laugh when you feel like you have to fart. I don't deserve to spend the second half of my life miserable, frustrated, and helpless about my body. So that's the reason why I got a Mini Tummy Tuck! I deserve to feel and look like The Super Woman that I am.

So I decided to go through with it. I decided I was going to do it without judgment, guilt, or shame. Including and especially mine! The real name for the surgery is abdominoplasty with reconstructive muscles. Basically what they did was cut along my C-section, sew my abdominal muscles back together again tight like a corset, got rid of my scar tissue build up that created a bump from my C-section, cut away the excess skin, created a new hole for my belly button, pulled my skin down and sewed me back up again. VOILA! A flat belly, just like that! I know there's a lot more that goes into it. You're probably thinking: Well, what about the recovery time? Was it painful? Did you have a hard time getting back to normal? Let me just tell you this...the pain from someone asking me if I was pregnant when I wasn't, was far more excruciating than the pain from throwing up right after surgery. And that was fucking painful! I've basically forgotten all about the pain of the recovery, but I will never forget how awful it felt to look pregnant when you're not.

It was the best thing I've ever done for myself since the birth of my children, which ironically was the reason I needed to get this done in the first place. Since the surgery, I haven't been asked if I was pregnant once! I know that doesn't seem like a big thing to you, but I can't even begin to tell you how much of a great feeling it is. How wonderful it is not to be reminded by total strangers that every now and again, you have a belly that sticks out so much, it looks like you're having a baby!! Even better feeling than that is that I've been regular and I hardly ever feel bloated. I'm thrilled I'm not full of shit. My husband still thinks I'm full of shit, but he's psyched I'm not depressed all the time. I can't express how delighted I am I can't believe how amazing it feels to be flat down there! I will never see or feel the numbness of that lump through my yoga pants again! To finally, after all these years, have a flat belly is the most phenomenal feeling in the world, and I get to feel this way for the rest of my life! I throw on clothes one time and I'm done! NO MORE SPANX!! No more fidgeting with my shirts so it doesn't make me look like I'm pregnant. No more shopping for hours for that perfect shirt that will accentuate my waist, but not show my pouch. I can pack for a road trip quickly and lightly. I don't have to bring eight different shirts for an overnight trip because I'm afraid of how I'm going to feel or look the next day! My only wish is that I should have done it sooner! I should have done it sooner! Why didn't I do it sooner? #shouldhavedoneitsooner

Now, that's exactly why I decided to write this chapter and tell you my inner most secrets. Believe me when I say this was a secret. No one knows about my tummy tuck, not even Howard Stern! So, telling you this is really terrifying for me because, now at this very moment, everyone knows. I'm putting myself out there and I'm sharing all this personal information with you because I want you to know that if you have ever felt like this and you're thinking about doing something like this, then do it!!! Don't wait another second. I don't want you to say I should have done it sooner!

I wrongly believed that it was vain, excessive, egotistical, ridiculous. Even my mother said to me that it was an unnecessary extreme. God forbid something goes wrong with the surgery and my husband had to explain to our boys, "You have no Mommy because she died trying to look thin!" So for the longest time I put it off and went back to my life feeling disgusted with myself. I continued to struggle with my body and I've learned to be comfortable with being uncomfortable and discouraged.

Until Howard Stern came into our lives, and my husband came into a little bit more money, and the guilt of spending money on this surgery just washed away just like that. I was lucky my husband and I had the means to let me go through with the surgery and that my husband was fully supportive and on board. Looking back now, I still shouldn't have waited for that moment. What if that moment never came? Where would I be? Still feeling miserable and life's too short for that! I'm here to tell you that I was lucky that moment came, but I'm writing this to tell you that it is important and it's not frivolous to want to be healthy and feel good about yourself. In hindsight, I didn't need Howard Stern to get the surgery. I should have found a way to do it. I shouldn't have put it off. I shouldn't have felt guilty. I should never have listened to my negative beliefs!

We should put ourselves number one on the list for once! We deserve it, but that's not what we do. Moms don't ever think about themselves. We put our health, happiness and well-being last. As Moms we need to take care of everyone else before we take care of ourselves. I feel good about myself now every day! That's priceless! Every morning I get up and I get dressed in seconds. I start off the day in a really great mood. You really can't put money on that.

Would you pay five bucks every morning to save time, look great in the first thing you put on, and start the day off with a huge smile, and have incredible confidence? Absolutely! Yet you would pay more than that at Starbucks every morning to get your high calorie, white chocolate mocha latte and stand in that long line to do it too!! Most of these doctors will put you on a payment plan so basically if you look at it, it's a car payment. So give up your coffee fix and drive around in a crappy car for a few years. Who cares, as long as you look good getting out of that shit box, nothing else matters.

No one knows about my tummy tuck. In fact most of family members and my closest friends are finding out now reading this for the first time. (I'm sorry I didn't tell you, I didn't tell anyone, I'm sorry, but I'm telling you now.) I wanted to share my story because a lot of women may have the same conflicting feelings as I did and I want to give them another perspective. Lots of women hide it, they don't talk about it. They want to keep it a secret because of lots of things, but it's mostly because others will judge you. So here I am spilling my guts out (literally) to you for the first time telling you I don't care what people think of me. They can judge me all they want, but I'm the only one who will define me, and I define me as Super Woman! If I help out just one person then this chapter will all be worth it! Whether it be plastic surgery, tummy tuck or any other elective surgery. Even if you may be thinking about any step towards making yourself feel good. Do it! Never feel guilty for doing it! Let me say this again, never feel guilty about doing it, and most importantly do it against all odds.

If you want something, go get it and don't let anyone stop you. My kids are so much better off with a happy mom! My kids don't even know I got this done! I better tell them before this book gets published. I'm a much better mom than I've ever dreamed of being. My husband is the most supportive man I've ever met and even he can't believe how incredibly happy I am. He had no idea how bad it was. He had no idea that I felt so incredibly ugly, uncomfortable, and depressed all that time and for all those years. He is so happy that I'm elated and that I can't stop smiling, which by the way will soon make my wrinkles stand out more, so now I have to get Botox. It's a never ending cycle. Don't worry about me, I'm not going to end up looking like that Cat Woman. I'm Super Woman, remember!

END OF YEAR REVIEW

MOMMY'S GOALS & OBJECTIVES

I will no longer go to the bathroom with an audience. I will NOT end my shower until I finish shaving my legs, deep conditioning my hair, and exfoliating my whole body.

I will not stop what I'm doing unless I hear:

"I'm on fire."

"Ryan Gosling's here."

Or "I'm bleeding profusely." ("I'm bleeding" alone will not stop me. It needs to be followed by "profusely." I will also accept "a lot," "it's gushing," or "I hit a vein.")

I will finish my morning coffee.

I will not feel guilty about letting my children eat a whole packet of butter, watch too much TV, or play violent video games.

Every Wednesday my children will get to choose their own dinner…Frosted Flakes or Pop Tarts.

When my children are screaming and fighting in the back seat of the car, I will turn my radio up and pretend I don't hear anything.

The next movie I see will be rated R or worse...I mean better.

Every time I say, "Keep your hands to yourself!" I will go back to my college drinking game days and make myself do a shot of vodka.

I will finish my afternoon coffee.

I will not care that I can't get my child to the birthday party on time. I embrace the fact that all the other mothers are looking at me like I'm the bad, disorganized mommy.

I will not do HOMEWORK! I refuse to feel dumb when I can't help my children do Common Core math.

The next time I forget to change over the laundry or I ask myself, "Why did I come into this room?" I will take that as a sure sign that I'm tired, overwhelmed and I will take a nap immediately.

I will not ignore my children while I go on Facebook and get depressed looking at all the wonderful things that other mothers are doing with their beautiful children.

The next time we go on vacation I will pack only for myself. Everyone else is on their own. Good Luck, Mommy loves you!

I will start clocking in my mommy hours. I will take all my sick days this year and demand a raise. All though I loved my bonus last year. The necklace made of tri-colored rigatoni. I demand that the bonus comes with stock options.

I will plan more play dates (aka "Girls Night Out").

I will make my children give me a 10 second hug at least once a day. I will do the counting. I will count by 1 Mississippi 2 Mississippi 3... I will refuse to let them let go until I get to 10. (This will seem like an eternity to a 10-year-old boy, but it will put a smile on my face.)

DON'T STOP BELIEVING...
WITHIN REASON!

So I didn't quit comedy after getting thrown up on by my children in front of industry bigwigs at the Montreal Comedy Festival, or after throwing up myself at a gig in an Atlantic City casino hotel room with my children after leaving them in "nighttime daycare," or after having a panic attack in a rest stop bathroom six months pregnant with twins. And I didn't quit comedy after coming home from a gig multiple times and paying my babysitter more than what I made that night. Why don't I just get a nice little part-time job at Starbucks – I hear they have good insurance. What is it about showbiz that just keeps me going? Sure this is the road not taken and I like being different, but if you put kids in the mix and a husband who's never home, then it's the road that no one should take. So why am I on it?

I'm constantly re-defining my passion for this business. I developed a webisode called "My Mommy Minute" then I wrote this book *Mean Mommy*. Why won't anyone just tell me to stop?! Oh yeah, they have... a million times! I'm just not listening. I guess it's because I grew up with my parents who always told me, "You can be anyone you want to be just as long as you work hard at it." I really believed them. "I can be anyone!" I thought.

Then as I grew older and I realized… it's a bunch of crap. I think my parents should have said to me, "You can be anyone you want to be as long as you work hard at it – WITHIN REASON!" But if they said "within reason" I probably wouldn't have even dreamed of trying to get into show business. I probably would have said to myself that's not within reason. I guess that's why I haven't gotten out of this unforgiving, judgmental, scathing, impossible career path. I guess it's because I believe. I believe it's possible against all odds. I believe I can do it, when everyone else has doubts, I believe in me. I've learned that's the most important thing. Believe you me, I wish I didn't believe in me. Life would be so much easier for me if I just stopped believing in myself. I wish I could be happy with mediocre, but I'm not. Then I get these doubts, that my very best might be someone's mediocre. These limiting beliefs come out to play, but they never stay long. They just pollute the air for a while and then somehow the air clears, like after a rain shower. Deep down inside of me, there is something that believes in me, time and time again. Then somehow, some way I get up again and that's what keeps me going. I know there are people out there laughing at me right now, "Look at her still going!" I don't care and I still believe. I told my family I was writing this book and they smiled and said politely, "Good luck. That's great." but I know they're thinking, "She can't even spell! She has dyslexia. What's she thinking?"

Yes, I know I have all those handicaps. But there's auto correct and Google! I love Google – it always knows what I'm trying to spell even if my attempt was so far off, somehow it knew what I was trying to do. I think Google has dyslexia, too. I love when it says, "Did you mean?"

"Yes, that's exactly what I meant! You know me better than my husband knows me, Google! I think I'm falling in love with you!"

Someone once asked me what the highlight of my career was. You know what came into my mind first? Not any of the TV shows I've gotten or any of the things I've been working so hard to achieve over the years. The first thing that came into my mind was the regular people that come up to me after a show and said, "Thank you so much of making me laugh. This is the first time I finally got out of the house since my divorce and I had a great time, and you made it all so worth it. Thank you!" Or the woman who came up to me and just brought me to tears as she was saying how wonderful it was to laugh again after all the chemo treatments she's had.

My favorite one was when a whole family came up to me to say that my show was their memorial tribute event for their father, because the very last time he laughed so hard was at my show. So they waited a little over a year until I got back to that club again and they got the whole family together to come see me. Can you believe that? I got a whole family to come together to celebrate, because I made their beloved father laugh. Those are the moments that carry me thought the next day. Those moments that make my hair stick up on the back of my neck, that make me cry in front of total strangers, that keep me from quitting. Those are the people who motivate me and these are my YES's. Find your YES's.

Wherever you go and whatever you do someone is going to tell you NO! There's always going to be someone who will try to push you down. There will always be someone stronger than you. Someone better than you. There will always be someone smarter, taller, thinner, prettier, and richer than you. There will be so many doors shut in your face and even more NO's! Until the no's become meaningless, but you will tell them, YES. And, if that doesn't work then, get a nose job!

This was the conversation the other night as I was putting my 8-year-old son to bed.

Mommy: Tommy, go to bed so I can go to work.

Tommy: You're not going to work, Mommy.

Mommy: Yes I am, I'm going to write my book.

Tommy: That's not a real job!

Mommy: Yes it is honey, now go to sleep!

I started to close the door.

Tommy: Mommy, wait! What job do you like the best?

Mommy: I like all of my jobs. Do you know what job is the hardest?

Tommy: What?

Mommy: Being a Mom! Do you know what job is the most important?

Tommy: What?

Mommy: Being a Mom! Do you know what job pays the least?

Tommy: Being a Mom?

Mommy: You're right, but do you know what's different about this job than any other job that's out there?

Tommy: No.

Mommy: This is the only job that no one could ever take my place. No one, nobody, no how, no way could anyone ever take the place of being your mom. No one, but ME! No one will ever love you like I love you!

Tommy: Wow, do you think I could be a Mom someday, too?

Mommy: Tommy, sweetheart, don't be silly. Of course, you can! You can be anyone you want to be, just as long as you work hard at it!

I may never reach my ultimate career goal, but I'm not going to stop trying. I'm not going to stop believing in myself. I'm going to continue to work really hard and be so good that at the very least, I will be proud of myself and that my kids will be proud of me, too. I will never stop believing in myself and I will never give up. Mostly, because I will be a good role model for my kids, and that will teach them to never stop believing in themselves. That's some mean stuff right there. Because I'm a *Mean Mommy*, my children will believe in themselves even more – and that's all that matters.

Mean Mommy was inspired by a poem called
How to be a Mean Mother (Author unknown).

How to be a Mean Mother

*A Mean Mother never allows candy or sweets to take the place of a
well-balanced meal.*
*A Mean Mother insists on knowing where her children are at all
times, who their friends are and what they do.*
*A Mean Mother breaks the child labor law by making her children
work washing dishes, making beds, learning to cook and doing other
cruel and unpleasant chores.*
*A Mean Mother makes life miserable for her offspring by insisting
that they always tell the truth.*
A Mean Mother produces teenagers who are wiser and more sensible.
*A Mean Mother can smile with secret delight and pride when she
hears her own grandchildren call their parents "Mean."*
What the world needs now is more Mean Mothers...and Fathers!

To read more bonus chapters by Kerri Louise,
visit KerriLouise.com or write to Kerri at
kerrilouise@kerrilouise.com.